Frontispiece   Cropmarks of a settlement near Kempsford. (N.M.R. Air Photograph: crown copyright)

The Committee for
Rescue Archaeology

in Avon, Gloucestershire
and Somerset

SURVEY No. 4

THE UPPER THAMES VALLEY
IN
GLOUCESTERSHIRE & WILTSHIRE
~
AN ARCHAEOLOGICAL SURVEY
OF THE RIVER GRAVELS

by
Roger Leech

COMMITTEE for RESCUE ARCHAEOLOGY in AVON, GLOUCESTERSHIRE & SOMERSET

PUBLICATIONS

General Editor: Dr Warwick Rodwell

SURVEYS

1. *Small Medieval Towns in Avon: Archaeology and Planning*
   Roger Leech (1975)

2. *Historic Towns in Somerset*
   Michael Aston and Roger Leech (1977)

3. *Historic Towns in Gloucestershire*
   Roger Leech, et al. (forthcoming)

4. *The Upper Thames Valley in Gloucestershire and Wiltshire: An Archaeological Survey of the River Gravels.*
   Roger Leech (1977)

EXCAVATION REPORTS

1. *Excavations in Bath, 1950–75*
   Barry Cunliffe, ed. (1977)

OCCASIONAL PAPERS

1. *Villages Survey: An Interim Report*
   Ann Ellison (1976)

2. *Newent Glasshouse*
   Alan G. Vince

Obtainable from:

CRAAGS, The Archaeological Centre, Mark Lane, Bristol 2

C. CRAAGS 1977
ISBN 0 904918 01 7

Photo-Lytho by HOLTON STUDIOS, CHELTENHAM
TEXT SET by GLOSTER DESIGN SERVICES (c&b) LTD. GLOUCESTER.
Printed by ALLEN GREEN, CHELTENHAM
DESIGNED AND PRODUCED by SABRA PUBLICATIONS, GLOUCESTER.

CONTENTS

		Page
List of illustrations		
Acknowledgements		
1.	Introduction	1
2.	Gravel Deposits	2
3.	Cropmarks: explanation and nature	3
4.	History	4
	4.1 Cropmarks and aerial photography	
	4.3 Excavation and fieldwork	
5.	Gazetteer	5
6.	Development factors affecting archaeological sites	19
	6.1 Gravel Extraction	
	6.3 Suburban expansion	
7.	Case Studies	20
	7.3 Area around Somerford Keynes	
	7.4 Area south of Fairford	
8.	Archaeological Provision	23
	8.2 Committee for Rescue Archaeology in Avon, Gloucestershire and Somerset	
	8.4 Corinium Museum, Cirencester	
	8.5 Wiltshire County Council, Libraries and Museums Service	
	8.6 Wiltshire Archaeological and Natural History Society	
	8.7 Conservation	
	8.8 Local Societies	
	8.9 National Organisations	
9.	Archaeology, legislation and planning	25
10.	Archaeological problems and potential	26
	10.1 General problems	
	10.4 Problems relating to particular periods.	
11.	Preservation, survey and excavation	27
	11.1 Preservation	
	11.3 Survey	
	11.4 Excavation	
12.	Recommendations	28
	12.1 Legislation and Planning	
	12.3 Archaeological Policy	
	12.8 Conclusion	
Appendix	Site grading and preservation	29
References	... ...	32

LIST OF ILLUSTRATIONS

Figures and Maps   **Page**

Fig. 1   The area covered by the survey   1
Fig. 2   Drift geology and incidence of cropmarks   2
Fig. 3   Key to cropmark maps   6
Map 1   Cropmarks around Cirencester   9
Map 2   Cropmarks around Somerford Keynes   10
Map 3   Cropmarks around Down Ampney   13
Map 4   Cropmarks south of Fairford   14
Map 5   Cropmarks around Lechlade   16
Map 6   Cropmarks south of Kempsford   18
Fig. 4   Past and future destruction of cropmarks around Somerford Keynes   21
Fig. 5   Past and future destruction of cropmarks south of Fairford   22

Plates

Frontispiece   Cropmarks of a settlement near Kempsford
Plate 1   Cropmarks of settlements between Fairford and Lechlade
Plate 2   Cropmarks at Street Farm, Latton
Plate 3   Cropmarks of a Romano-British settlement at Field Barn, Latton
Plate 4   Cropmarks near Alex Farm, Latton
Plate 5   Cropmarks of rectangular enclosures north of Latton
Plate 6   Cropmarks of ring ditches and ridge and furrow near Castle Eaton
Plate 7   Excavations at Lechlade, 1961
Plate 8   Cropmarks of a Romano-British settlement at Paradise Farm, Lechlade

ACKNOWLEDGEMENTS

This survey could not have been compiled without the great assistance given by the Royal Commission on Historical Monuments (England), and much of the archaeological information for Gloucestershire has been taken directly from the RCHM Inventory *Iron Age and Romano-British Monuments in the Cotswold Area.* The plotting of the cropmarks for Wiltshire has been partly undertaken by Dr. I.F. Smith, of the Commission's staff, and partly by L. Thompson of CRAAGS.

Much assistance in the preparation of this survey has been given by the Planning Departments of Gloucestershire and Wiltshire County Councils, and Cotswold and North Wiltshire District Councils. Advice on archaeological matters has been given by D. Viner (Corinium Museum) and W.J. Ford and R.A. Canham (Wiltshire County Council), and many other persons have assisted in various ways, including: H.C. Bowen, B.N. Eagles, P.J. Fowler, C.J. Gingell, J.E. Hancock, Miss V.S. Hill, Mrs. P.C. Leech, Mrs. D. Parker, W.J. Rodwell, R.D. Savage, M. Stone, Mrs. V. Swan and B. Walters. I am also grateful to H.C. Bowen, Dr. J.M. Coles, N. Thomas and Dr, I.F. Smith for reading and commenting on the draft of the text.

All maps are based on Ordnance Survey plans with the sanction of the Controller of H.M. Stationery Office; Crown Copyright reserved.

The following have kindly given permission to reproduce their copyright photographs: A. Baker (Pl. 7), the National Monuments Record (Frontispiece, Pl.5, 8), Professor J.K. St. Joseph (Pl. 1), M. Stone (Pl. 3,4,6) and B. Walters (Pl. 2).

1. INTRODUCTION

1.1 This Survey has been commissioned by the Directorate of Ancient Monuments and Historic Buildings (Department of the Environment) through the Committee for Rescue Archaeology in Avon, Gloucestershire and Somerset. The survey is a contribution to the overall assessment of the archaeological implications of gravel extraction in the Upper Thames Valley. At the request of the Ancient Monuments Inspectorate, the report is intentionally of similar format to that recently published for the Upper Thames Valley in Oxfordshire (Benson and Miles 1974), and to a comparable report on the river gravels in Berkshire (Gates, 1975). Sections Two, Three and Eleven here closely follow the Oxfordshire Survey.

1.2. The present survey relies heavily on the work of the Royal Commission on Historical Monuments (England), which has generously allowed CRAAGS to use much of its own material in advance of publication. Cropmarks in Gloucestershire are plotted from illustrations which will appear in the RCHM inventory on the Gloucestershire Cotswolds and those in Wiltshire are in part traced from a map prepared by Dr Isobel Smith. The gazetteer for Gloucestershire is based on the RCHM text.

1.3 Many of the sites shown on the maps have already been destroyed and many more lie within areas designated for gravel extraction. The unrecorded destruction of archaeological sites may be likened to the burning of historic manuscripts which have never been read. It is hoped that this survey will increase awareness of the need for detailed archaeological investigation in the Upper Thames Valley in Gloucestershire and Wiltshire.

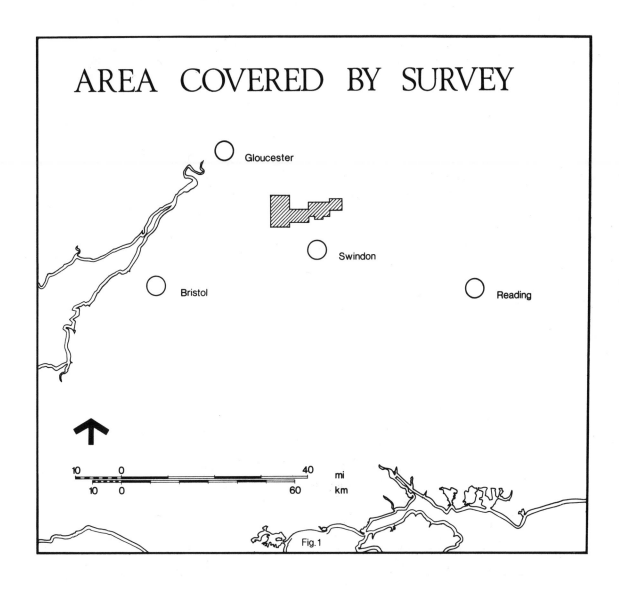

AREA COVERED BY SURVEY

Gloucester

Swindon

Bristol

Reading

10   0   40   mi

10   0   60   km

Fig.1

1.4   The survey arises out of two earlier publications. The Cotswold Water Park (Cotswold Water Park Joint Committee 1969) outlined future planning proposals for gravel extraction in the Upper Thames Valley in Gloucestershire and Wiltshire, and showed how extraction would be related to hydrology, transportation, landscape, recreation, places of interest and wildlife conservation. No mention was made of the archaeological richness of the area or of its absolute destruction in the course of gravel extraction.

A Penny for your Past (Gingell 1971) expressed the local archaeological reaction to this situation; it emphasised the urgent need for the archaeological investigation of sites about to be destroyed and its various recommendations included that 'a qualified and experienced archaeologist by appointed by the Cotswold Water Park Joint Committee'. In the event no official response was forthcoming, and no detailed investigation of the sites being destroyed has taken place between 1971 and the present.

1.5   A second planning report, Plan for the River Thames, Lechlade to Cricklade (Gloucestershire and Wiltshire County Councils 1971), arose from surveys initially carried out in the 1960s. Although this considered the historical environment, it showed no real awareness of the archaeological dimensions, referring only to Scheduled Ancient Monuments (9.5).

1.6   This present survey should be regarded only as an interim and minimal statement of the archaeological potential of the Upper Thames river gravels, and because it is intended to be studied alongside the Oxfordshire Survey (Benson and Miles 1974), sites other than cropmarks are but briefly mentioned. For the medieval period especially, only a more detailed survey would provide a comprehensive picture. Future air reconnaissance will also increase our knowledge of cropmark sites of all periods.

1.7   The survey is set out in a series of sections and paragraphs and cross-references are given in the form (3.2). The illustrations accompanying the gazetteer are referred to as Maps; all other illustrations as Figs. or Plates.

2.   GRAVEL DEPOSITS

2.1   The gravels of the Upper Thames Valley (Fig. 2) are the result of the deposition of largely calcareous material, derived from the northern limestone, washed down by the rivers of an earlier Upper Thames system. The present fragmented distribution of these deposits is due to changes in the course of the river, combined with successive lowerings of its bed, leaving the gravel isolated in terraced form. The glacial plateau gravels, which have a wider and generally higher distribution, have not been considered in this survey.

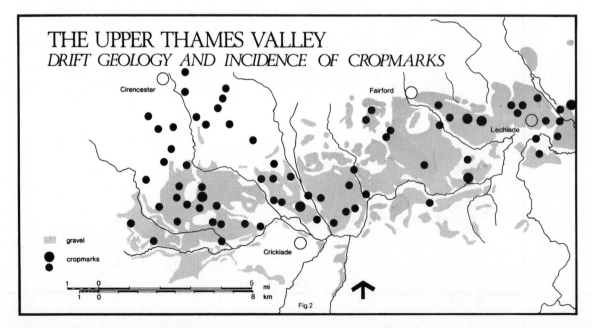

THE UPPER THAMES VALLEY
DRIFT GEOLOGY AND INCIDENCE OF CROPMARKS

Cirencester
Fairford
Lechlade

gravel
cropmarks

Cricklade

1   0   5   mi
1   0   8   km

Fig. 2

2.2   There is evidence for preferential occupation of the river gravel terraces by early settlers, but detailed discussion of this is not appropriate here. On the whole, present-day exploitation of the gravel deposits is not confined to any one terrace, nor is likely to be in the future. The lower terraces however, being more extensive than the rest, have generally been preferred for large-scale extraction.

2.3   The survey is confined to the traces of Man's occupation on the gravels after the formation of all the terraces and when the landscape had broadly assumed its present form. It is worth noting however that even during this period of formation, Man was present in the region. His remains, principally flint tools and bones of the fauna upon which he was so dependent, occur within the gravel deposits themselves, as a result of much re-distribution and re-sorting at the time when the terraces were laid down. It is a matter for regret and concern that, in the large-scale quarrying of these terraces, the archaeological finds and information on the geomorphology of the gravels have not been sought or recorded adequately in recent decades, nor are they yet receiving the attention they deserve.

3.   CROPMARKS: EXPLANATION AND NATURE

3.1   The cropmarks which are illustrated in the gazetteer are the result of differential growth (usually of cereals), reflecting the existence of buried features of which, generally, no surface traces remain. The process which leads to the formation of cropmarks is complicated and ill-understood: the explanation presented here is, of necessity, oversimplified. Ditches or pits dug into the gravel in former times will silt up and provide a localised reservoir of deeper, and often richer, soil. These pockets of deep soil retain moisture and encourage deep root development and so stimulate extra growth in the crops and prolong their ripening. Thus, cereals growing over buried archaeological features may stand out as taller and greener than the adjacent crop.

Gravel subsoils are particularly suitable for the observation of cropmarks because, being well drained, in a period of dry weather the difference in moisture content between the normal soils and those over deep pockets is relatively great, and colour differences in the crop are consequently well marked. For a crop to reflect these soil pockets, it is necessary that it should be one with a deep root development - thus barley will show cropmarks, but grass or rootcrops will not, except in very unusual circumstances. Areas of thick, greener crop over deep features may be termed 'positive cropmarks'.

Where there are buried stony features, such as walls or roads, different phenomena may be observed. Here, the crop is starved of moisture and nutrients and its root development limited. In such cases we may see 'negative cropmarks' or parchmarks appearing, representing areas of weak crop growth acompanied by relatively rapid ripening.

Infilled ditches, now visible only as cropmarks, would often have had associated earthworks, for example burial mounds or enclosure banks. These have now usually been flattened by ploughing, so that it is only from the cropmarks over their ditches that the presence of such archaeological sites can be recognised. Cropmarks can most effectively be observed from an aircraft since although they can sometimes be seen at ground level, it is extremely difficult to interpret their pattern.

3.2   As a result of excavation, and by comparison with examples of upstanding monuments elsewhere, individual cropmarks can sometimes be assigned to specific periods or classified as particular types of site. Some circles, for example, represent ditches around ploughed - out burial mounds, generally of the second millennium B.C., whilst others may represent enclosures for domestic or agricultural purposes. Fainter and less complete circles may represent drainage ditches around circular timber huts whose postholes, usually too slight to show as cropmarks, can only be recovered by excavation. Rectilinear enclosures may represent parts of farmsteads, perhaps of the later prehistoric or Roman periods. These enclosures are often associated with pairs of long parallel lines which may, in some cases, represent trackways. They form a pattern which resembles that made by our village lanes and streets today. Clusters of dark spots can indicate the presence of pits, originally often used for grain storage or refuse disposal. These are usually of the late first millennium B.C., whilst some of the less obtrusive markings may be much earlier. Sunken floored huts (Grubenhäuser) associated with early Saxon settlements are sometimes recognisable as dark spots but tend to be larger and more rectilinear than cropmarks of individual pits.

3.3   The number of known sites in the Upper Thames Valley (Fig. 2) in no way represents the true density of settlement. The absence of cropmarks in many areas may be caused by lack of aerial survey, unsuitable crop at the time of survey, or by the fact that some land is still under pasture, a condition unsuitable for producing cropmarks. In the area around Down Ampney (Map 3) over half the cropmarks plotted were observed for the first time in 1975, underlining the need for continued air survey.

3.4   Several cropmark features which appear on aerial photographs do not seem to be man-made; amongst these are marks of periglacial origin, for example ice wedges and frost cracks (Evans 1972, Williams 1973). These are particularly common on the second and third terraces, and also on the plateau gravel (Riley 1944, 83). In many cases they have, nevertheless, been plotted on the maps in this survey, since it is sometimes difficult to distinguish them from man-made linear features.

4.   HISTORY

Cropmarks and Aerial Photography

4.1   The history of air photography in the Upper Thames Valley has been summarised in the Oxfordshire Survey (Benson and Miles 1974, 19-20). Cropmarks were noted long before the invention of the aeroplane, and were even surveyed at ground level for Haverfield in 1897. In the 1920s and '30s the pioneer air photography of Beazeley and Crawford was followed by the work of Major G.W. Allen and subsequently by that of Flying Officer D.N. Riley. Since 1945 air photography has been extensively undertaken by Professor J.K. St. Joseph, Mr. A. Baker and the National Monuments Record.

4.2   Until the late 1960s no overall assessment of the results of air photography in the Upper Thames Valley was made. Ideally, such an assessment should be made on a broad archaeological basis taking into consideration areas beyond the limits of the gravels. Such an approach has been adopted by the RCHM for their forthcoming Gloucestershire volume. The Royal Commission is now surveying Wiltshire, for which an inventory will be published in due course.
This survey and the comparable volumes for Oxfordshire and Berkshire provide assessments of the gravels and immediately adjacent areas only. They should be seen as emergency documents compiled in the face of rapid gravel extraction, and in particular, highlighting the importance of sites that may well be destroyed before the publication of the relevant Royal Commission inventories.

Excavation and Fieldwork

4.3   In the Oxfordshire region, excavations on gravel sites threatened with destruction have taken place almost annually since c.1930 (Benson and Miles 1974, 20-22). Although many of these excavations were on a very limited scale, much useful research has nevertheless been undertaken, which may in part have been stimulated by the proximity of a University and a County Museum (Gingell 1971, 9). Since 1968 a series of more extensive excavations has been carried out; they are listed in the following table. The contrast with the single excavation on gravel in the Water Park Area of Gloucestershire and Wiltshire in the same period needs no further emphasis.

Year	Oxfordshire	Gloucestershire & Wiltshire
1968	New Wintles Farm, Eynsham	—
1969	Long Wittenham	—
1970	—	—
1971	New Wintles Farm, Eynsham	Ashton Keynes, Glos.
	Barton Court Farm, Abingdon	—
1972	Barton Court Farm, Abingdon	—
	Devils Quoits, Stanton Harcourt	—
1973	Barton Court Farm, Abingdon	—
	Wilsham Road, Abingdon	—
	Appleford	—
	Devils Quoits, Stanton Harcourt	—

(cont)

1974	Barton Court Farm, Abingdon	–
	Wally Corner, Berinsfield	–
	Ashville Trading Estate, Abingdon	–
1975	Barton Court Farm, Abingdon	–
	Wally Corner, Berinsfield	–
	Farmoor	–

(Ministry of Public Building & Works 1969, 1970; Department of the Environment 1971, 1972, 1973, 1974).

All the above excavations were carried out on behalf of the (now) Department of the Environment; none has yet been fully published.

4.4   Only two sites in the Cotswold Water Park have ever been examined in detail. The first was at Roughground Farm, Lechlade, Gloucestershire, where extensive excavations directed by Mrs. M.U. Jones were carried out between 1958 and 1965 on an Iron Age and Romano-British settlement now completely quarried away (RCHM Lechlade (5)). The second was at Ashton Keynes, Wiltshire, where a limited excavation was directed by Dr. I.A. Kinnes in 1971 on the site of a Romano-British enclosure, now also quarried away (4.4). Both these excavations were undertaken on behalf of the Department of the Environment, and neither has yet been fully published.

4.5   The modest amount of archaeological research on the river gravels of Gloucestershire and Wiltshire may be contrasted with the many excavations in nearby Cirencester.

4.6   The second largest Roman town in Britain, Cirencester has been a major focus of archaeological attention over the last two decades. Many areas within the limits of the Roman town have been built on for the first time since the Roman period and this, added to central redevelopment, has necessitated much rescue excavation; since 1957 nineteen seasons of excavation have been carried out, largely financed by the Department of the Environment (Richmond & Taylor 1958-60; Richmond & Wilson 1961; Wilson 1962-74). The first two seasons of excavation have been published in full (Webster 1969; Rennie 1971); and preparations for the publication of the remaining seventeen seasons are in hand.

4.7   There have also been a number of regional studies based partly on excavations and partly on other research. For example, Bronze Age barrows and ring ditches have been examined closely (O' Neill & Grinsell 1960; Smith 1972), and various types of site were given extensive treatment in 1960 (RCHM 1960). Particular periods examined in detail have included the Iron Age (Harding 1972) and the Anglo-Saxon (Myres 1969). The only overall studies of the area covered by this survey have been in the Victoria County History of Wiltshire (Bonney 1973; Cunliffe 1973; Piggot 1973) and the RCHM Inventory for Gloucestershire. By the very nature of their brief, neither has been able to give a truly regional study of the Upper Thames Valley, situated as it is astride the boundary between two counties.

5.   GAZETTEER

5.1   As previously emphasised (3.3), the list of cropmarks in the Gazetteer should be regarded as an interim statement only. The fact that certain areas in the region are not covered by any of the following maps should not be taken to imply that no sites exist there. Indeed, it is probable that cropmarks will be discovered in those areas in the future.

5.2   The Gazetteer consists of maps accompanied by a textual description. All maps are drawn to coincide with numbered National Grid Kilometre squares, and the key (Fig. 3) shows the areas covered. Many cropmarks are plotted directly from RCHM plans or from Dr. Isobel Smith's plan. Sites not visible as cropmarks but of likely prehistoric or Roman date are shown as red circles (small sites) or as red stipple (sites of larger extent). Ermine Street and the Fosse Way, the main Roman roads, are also marked in red. A few notable medieval sites have been marked in black, but, as noted above (1.6), no thorough coverage of the medieval archaeology of the area has been undertaken.

5

5.3 Bibliographical references in the Gazetteer have been limited. A lengthy bibliography could be produced, particularly where excavations have taken place, but would be of dubious value in the present context.

Air Photographs

5.4 The sources for these are as follows:

ALLEN   Photographs taken by the late Major G.W.G. Allen. Ashmolean Museum, Oxford, and N.M.R.

BAKER   Photographs taken by A. Baker. Collection held by N.M.R. and Birmingham University.

CRAAGS   Photographs taken by J.E. Hancock for the Committee for Rescue Archaeology in Avon, Gloucestershire & Somerset.

CUAP   Photographs taken mainly by Professor J.K. St. Joseph and D.R. Wilson for the University of Cambridge Committee for Aerial Photography.

FAIREY   Photographs taken by Fairey Surveys Ltd., Maidenhead, Berkshire.

NMR   Photographs taken by, or under the direction of, J.N. Hampton, National Monuments Record, Air Photograph Unit, London.

OS   Photographs taken for the Ordnance Survey, Southampton.

STONE   Photographs taken by M. Stone, Highworth. Copies of some held by CRAAGS.

WALTERS   Photographs taken by B. Walters, Swindon, Wiltshire.

WILTS   Photographs held by the Planning Department, Wiltshire County Council.

Abbreviations

5.5 (Apart from bibliographical references)

OAP   Oblique air photograph.

OS/SP, OS/SU   Reference to the card index of sites, Archaeology Division, Ordnance Survey.

VAP   Vertical air photograph.

Wilts CC   Sites and Monuments Record, Wiltshire County Council.

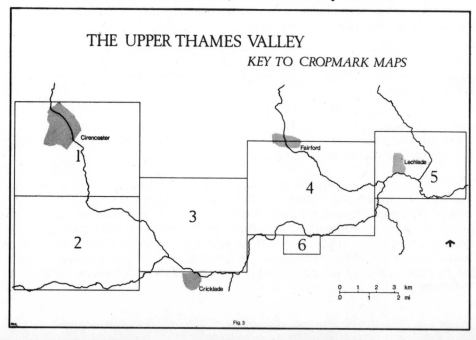

Fig. 3

MAP 1

0100/0199 SP 00 SW SU 09 NW Area centred SU 017997
CIRENCESTER and SIDDINGTON, GLOUCESTERSHIRE
Ploughed up debris indicates Romano-British buildings.
Cropmarks extend over about 15 hectares.
RCHM, Cirencester (3)
        Siddington (1)
CUAP OAP A00 45—6, AOS 10—11, ASM 47

0101/0201/0202/0301/0302 SP 00 SW Area centred
SP 025018
CIRENCESTER, GLOUCESTERSHIRE
Roman town and cemeteries.
RCHM, Cirencester

0102 SP 00 SW Area centred SP 016025
CIRENCESTER, GLOUCESTERSHIRE
Spread of occupation debris indicating Romano-British
settlement.
RCHM, Cirencester (2)

0102 SP 00 SW SP 016023
CIRENCESTER, GLOUCESTERSHIRE
Romano-British villa, partially excavated in 1824, 1909
and 1937.
RCHM, Cirencester (1)

0298 SU 09 NW Area centred SU 028988
SIDDINGTON, GLOUCESTERSHIRE
Spread of occupation and building debris indicating
Romano-British settlement.
RCHM, Siddington (3)

0298 SU 09 NW Area centred SU 021984
SIDDINGTON, GLOUCESTERSHIRE
Probable settlement faintly indicated by cropmarks
over an area of about 1 hectare.
RCHM, Siddington (7)
CUAP OAP AZN 43

0298 SU 09 NW SU 029983
SIDDINGTON, GLOUCESTERSHIRE
Rectangular enclosure, undated.
CRAAGS OAP SU 0298/A (J.E. Hancock)

0298/0398 SU 09 NW Area centred SU 031984
SIDDINGTON, GLOUCESTERSHIRE
Ring ditch and trackway, undated, the latter of a width
to suggest a drove, along the bottom of a shallow valley
beside a brook.
RCHM, Siddington (4)
NMR OAP SU 0398/2/372—6

0299 SU 09 NW Area centred SU 021993
SIDDINGTON, GLOUCESTERSHIRE
Enclosures, undated, SW of Ewen Bridge are partly
visible as cropmarks on level ground. The SE side of the
larger enclosure is about 55m long.
RCHM, Siddington (2)
CUAP OAP A00 44, ASM 45

0299 SU 09 NW SU 02939932
SIDDINGTON, GLOUCESTERSHIRE
Rectilinear ditches, undated, NW of the Quarries,
defining three parallel strips each about 21 m across.
RCHM, Siddington (8)
NMR OAP SU 0299/1/377

0299 SU 09 NW SU 02999941
SIDDINGTON, GLOUCESTERSHIRE
Double ring ditch. The inner ditch appears to enclose a
central circular mark about 3 m across.
Smith 1972, 163

0301/0302 SP 00 SW Area centred SP 037020
CIRENCESTER, GLOUCESTERSHIRE
Enclosures and probable settlement are visible over an
area of about 14 hectares.
RCHM, Cirencester (5)
CUAP OAP AOO 33—4
NMR OAP SP 0302/2/265—72, 0302/4/338—41

0301 SP 00 SW Area centred SP 036012
PRESTON, GLOUCESTERSHIRE
Cropmarks of linear features and enclosures extend over
about 5 hectares.
RCHM, Preston (1)
NMR OAP SP 0300/1/332—3, 0301/2/334—7

0400 SP 00 SW SP 04500033
PRESTON, GLOUCESTERSHIRE
Ring ditch.
OS/SP/00/SW 45

0400/0499 SP 00 SW SU 09 NW
Area centred SU 047997
SIDDINGTON, GLOUCESTERSHIRE
Ploughed out Romano-British settlement on Worm's
Farm adjacent to Ermine Street shows in the form of
cropmarks over some 12 hectares and as a spread of
occupation debris on a more limited area. The N part of
the settlement is on level ground, the rest lies on a slope
facing S. The cropmarks suggest reorganisation of
boundaries within the settlement.
Linear ditches 275 m to the N (SU 044000) are undated.
RCHM, Siddington (6)
CUAP OAP AOR98, ASM 51—2, 55, AXO 93

0499 SU 09 NW SU 04279974
SIDDINGTON, GLOUCESTERSHIRE.
Ring ditch.
OS/SU/09/NW/29

0500 SP 00 SE Area centred SP 054006
PRESTON, GLOUCESTERSHIRE
Enclosures and linear ditches, undated, W of
St. Augustine's Farm.
RCHM, Preston (2)
CUAP OAP A00 31—2
NMR OAP SP 0500/3/263—4, 0500/5/177—8

0501 SP 00 SE Area centred SP 05700115
PRESTON, GLOUCESTERSHIRE
Enclosures, undated, N of St. Augustine's Farm.
RCHM, Preston (3)
CUAP OAP A00 31, ASM 57

0598 SU 09 NW SU 05939848
SOUTH CERNEY, GLOUCESTERSHIRE
Ring ditch.
OS/SU/09/NE 15
BAKER SU 0598/3 1969

0598 SU 09 NE Area centred SU 053986
SOUTH CERNEY, GLOUCESTERSHIRE
Enclosure and parallel ditches, undated.
RCHM, South Cerney (1)
NMR OAP SU 0598/1/169−72

0598 SU 09 NE SU 05599830
SOUTH CERNEY, GLOUCESTERSHIRE
Rectangular enclosure, undated, with a gap in the S side.
RCHM, South Cerney (2)
CUAP OAP AYG 42

0598/0698 SU 09 NE SU 063979
SOUTH CERNEY, GLOUCESTERSHIRE
Trackway with enclosures to the S (see Map 2), undated.
RCHM, South Cerney (3)
CUAP OAP AYG 40−1
NMR OAP SU 0697/5

0599/0699 SU 09 NE Area centred SU 059996
DRIFFIELD, GLOUCESTERSHIRE
Enclosures, linear ditches and ring ditch, undated.
RCHM, Driffield (2)
NMR OAP SU 0599/1

0602 SP 00 NE Area centred SP 069031
AMPNEY CRUCIS, GLOUCESTERSHIRE
Probable settlement S of Akeman Street, revealed by cropmarks covering 12 hectares of Forest Marble (mainly to the N of Map 1).
ACHM, Ampney Crucis (1)
CUAP OAP AOS 22−3

MAP 2

0094 SU 09 SW SU 008945
POOLE KEYNES, GLOUCESTERSHIRE
Wide track and enclosure, undated.
RCHM, Poole Keynes (1)
OS VAP 70/042/132

0193/0293 SU 09 SW Area centred SU 021936
SOMERFORD KEYNES, GLOUCESTERSHIRE
Probable settlement between the Swill Brook and Flagham Brook over an area of some 14 hectares. Two fragments of samian ware, now in Gloucester City Museum, came from the SW part of the complex.
RCHM, Somerford Keynes (1)
NMR OAP SP 0293/1/388−9, 0293/2/390−1

0194 SU 09 SW Area centred SU 019945
SOMERFORD KEYNES, GLOUCESTERSHIRE
Probable settlement, undated, 185 m S of the Thames at Neigh Bridge shows indistinctly as a dense complex of cropmarks covering some 2.5 hectares. Multiple linear ditches divide the area into approximately rectangular plots, within which are indications of D-shaped and sub-circular enclosures.
RCHM, Somerford Keynes (2)
OS VAP 70/030/132

0196 SU 09 NW Area centred SU 016968
SOMERFORD KEYNES' GLOUCESTERSHIRE
Probable settlement, undated, shows over some 7 hectares of level ground. The internal area of the double-ditched enclosure is about one quarter of a hectare.
RCHM, Somerford Keynes (4)
CRAAGS OAP SU 0196/A (J.E. Hancock)
OS VAP 70/042/158
NMR OAP SU 0196/1/383−5

0196 SU 09 NW Area centred SU 019969
SOMERFORD KEYNES, GLOUCESTERSHIRE
Part of an oval enclosure and linear features, probably a continuation of the settlement at SU 016968 (above).
CRAAGS OAP SU 0196/A (J.E. Hancock)

0294 SU 09 SW SU 02719485
SOMERFORD KEYNES, GLOUCESTERSHIRE
Ring ditch.
BAKER SU 0294/2 1965, 0294/1 204

0294/0394 SU 09 SW Area centred SU 032947
SOMERFORD KEYNES, GLOUCESTERSHIRE and ASHTON KEYNES, WILTSHIRE
Romano-British settlement, partly excavated by Dr.I.A. Kinnes in 1971. Cropmarks plotted by Dr. I.F. Smith in 1971.
RCHM, Somerford Keynes (6)
Department of the Environment 1972, 23
CUAP OAP AYG 38
NMR OAP SU 0394/5/393−5

0295 SU 09 SW Area centred SU 025957
SOMERFORD KEYNES, GLOUCESTERSHIRE
Enclosure and linear ditches, undated, W of Spratsgate Lane, show as indistinct cropmarks now partly destroyed by gravel digging. The complex includes a rectangular enclosure, probably beside a track.
RCHM, Somerford Keynes (3)
NMR OAP BAKER SU 0295/1

0295 SU 09 NW SU 023953
SOMERFORD KEYNES, GLOUCESTERSHIRE
Subrectangular enclosure, undated.
CRAAGS OAP SU 0295/A (J.E. Hancock)

0295/0296/0395/0396 SU 09 NW SU 09 SW
Area centred SU 031958
SOMERFORD KEYNES, GLOUCESTERSHIRE and ASHTON KEYNES, WILTSHIRE
Linear ditches, trackway and ring ditches, undated, cropmarks plotted by Dr. I.F. Smith in 1971.
CUAP AOR 99, AXO 89, AYB 71

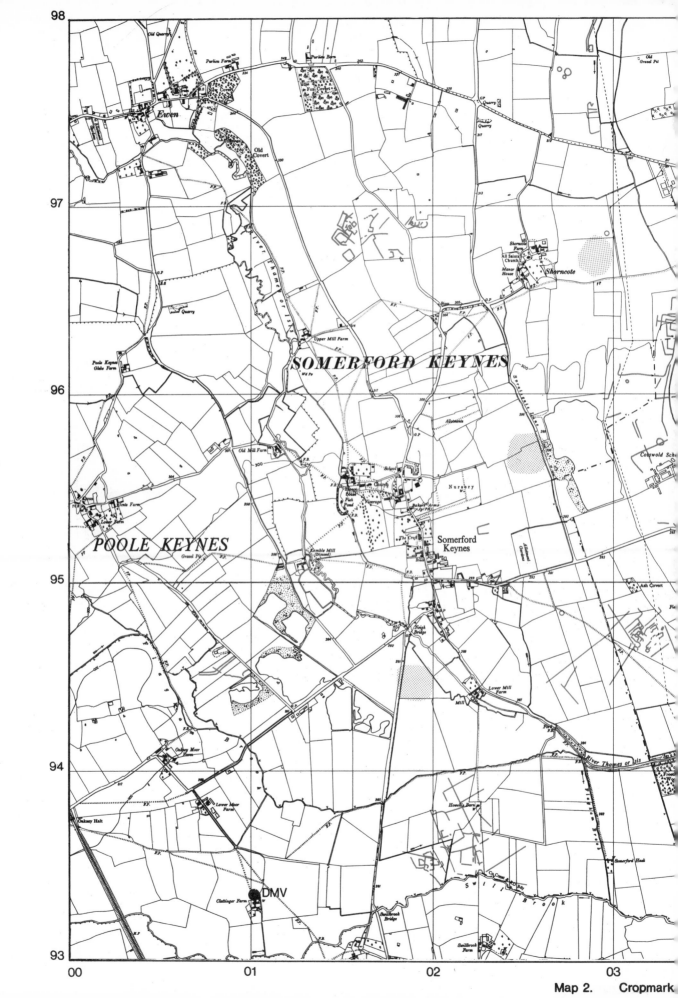

Map 2.   Cropmark

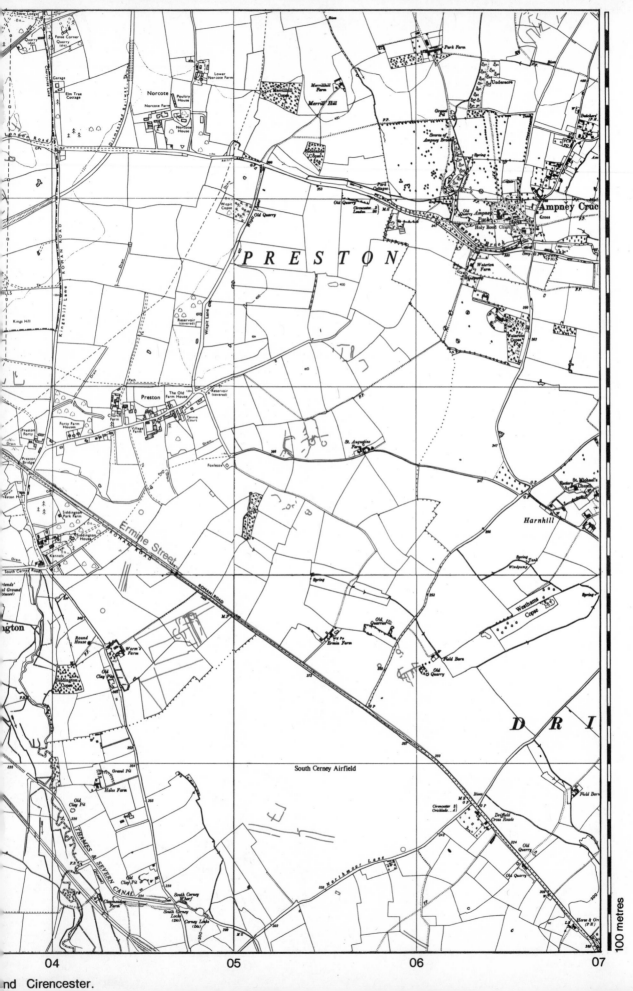

P R E S T O N

Ampney Cruc

Harnhill

D R I

Norcote

Kings Hill

Preston

Ermine Street

Siddington Park Farm

Round House

Worm's Farm

South Cerney Airfield

THAMES & SEVERN CANAL

100 metres

04   05   06   07

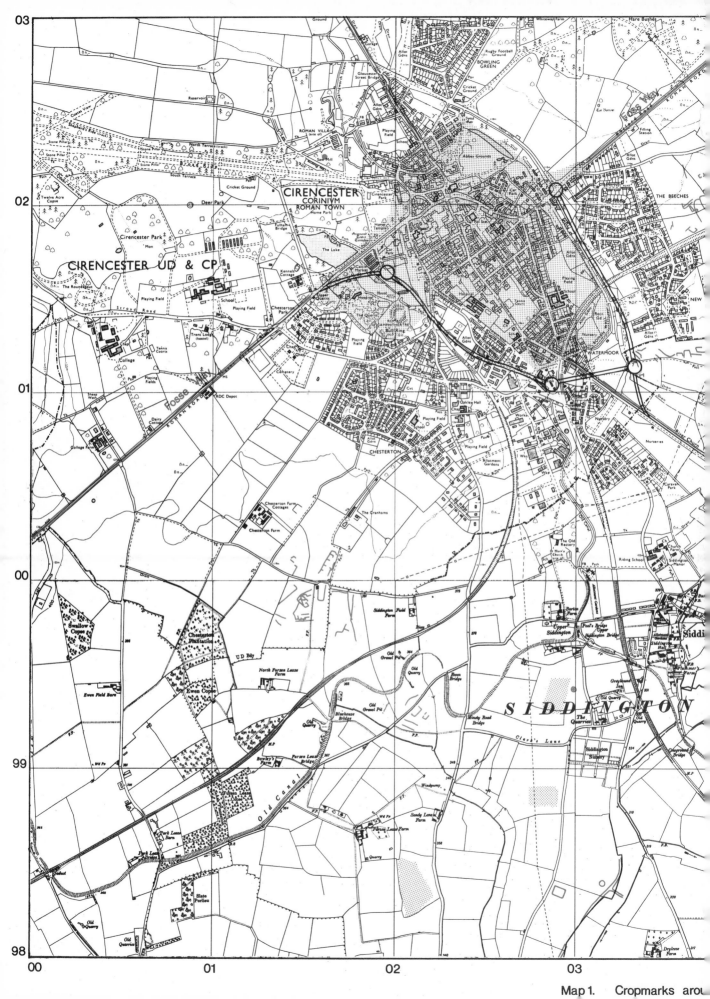

Map 1.   Cropmarks aroun

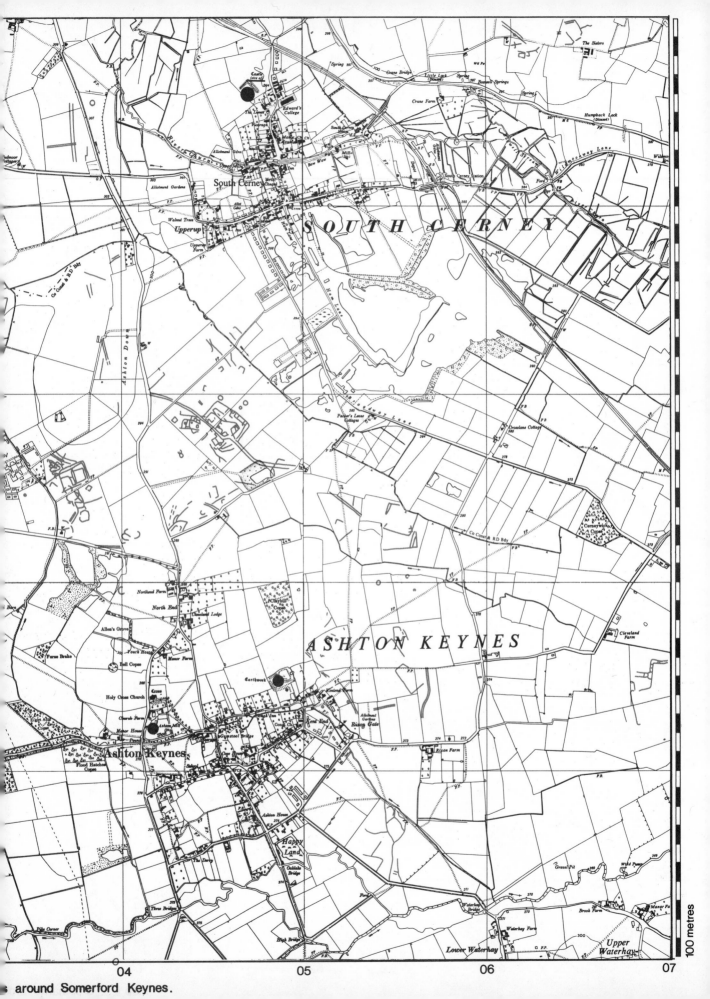

around Somerford Keynes.

0296 SU 09 NW Area centred SU 029967
SOMERFORD KEYNES, GLOUCESTERSHIRE
Ring ditch and linear ditches, undated, are revealed by
indistinct cropmarks E of Shorncote.
RCHM, Somerford Keynes (5)
OS VAP 70/042/159
NMR OAP SU 0396/1/110—11

0297 SU 09 NW Area centred SU 031984 (see map 1)
SIDDINGTON, GLOUCESTERSHIRE
Enclosure, trackway and ring ditches, undated, W of
Dryleaze Farm.
RCHM, Siddington (4)
Smith 1972, 159
NMR OAP SU 0398/2/372—6

0297 SU 09 NW Area centred SU 028975
SIDDINGTON, GLOUCESTERSHIRE
Enclosure, undated. The W side is about 150 m long and
there are internal subdivisions.
RCHM, Siddington (5)
NMR OAP SU 0297/7/381

0393 SU 09 SW SU 03959300
ASHTON KEYNES, WILTSHIRE
Ring ditch. Cropmark plotted by Dr. I.F. Smith
OS VAP 70/030/104

0395 SU 09 NW Area centred SU 037956
ASHTON KEYNES, WILTSHIRE
Settlement with trackways and rectangular enclosures,
undated. Cropmarks plotted by Dr. I.F. Smith in 1971.
CUAP OAP AXO 92, AYB 70, 73
NMR OAP SU 0395/1 (D.N. Riley), SU 0395/2/396—7
OS VAP 70/042/145—6, 160—1

0396 SU 09 NW Area centred SU 031965
SOMERFORD KEYNES, GLOUCESTERSHIRE and
ASHTON KEYNES, WILTSHIRE
Settlement with trackways and at least 5 rectangular
enclosures, undated.
CRAAGS OAP 0396/A/B (J.E. Hancock)

0396 SU 09 NW Area centred on SU 038965
ASHTON KEYNES, WILTSHIRE
Linear features and trackway, undated. Cropmarks
plotted by Dr. I.F. Smith in 1971.
NMR OAP SU 0396-7

0397 SU 09 NW SU 037973
SIDDINGTON, GLOUCESTERSHIRE
Linear feature and trackway, undated.
CRAAGS OAP SU 0397/A (J.E. Hancock)

0397 SU 09 NW SU 038975
SIDDINGTON, GLOUCESTERSHIRE
Ring ditch, or possibly a circular enclosure with opposed
entrances, undated.
CRAAGS OAP SU 0397/B (J.E. Hancock)

0495/0496 SU 09 NW Area centred SU 045958
ASHTON KEYNES, WILTSHIRE
Settlement with rectangular and sub rectangular enclosures
on both sides of a trackway. Ring ditches are outside the
settlement area and beyond are isolated linear features
including trackways, undated.
Cropmarks plotted by Dr. I.F. Smith in 1971.
CUAP AOS 1—2, 13—14, ASM 84, 86
NMR SU 0495/8—11 (D.N. Riley), 0495/12/398—400,
0495/13/401—6 OS VAP 70/042/145—6

0593 SU 09 SE Area centred SU 055935
ASHTON KEYNES, WILTSHIRE
Linear features showing as soil marks.
OS VAP 70/030/107

0594 SU 09 SE Area centred SU 053956
ASHTON KEYNES, WILTSHIRE
Enclosures, linear features and ring ditches, undated. A
small enclosure with two buildings and an entrance on
the SE side is indicated at SU 05159470. Cropmarks
plotted by Dr. I.F. Smith in 1971.
CRAAGS OAP SU 0594/A (J.E. Hancock)
CUAP AOS 3, ASM 88, 93—4, AYB 78, AYG 39
NMR SU 0595/3, 0594/4/418—20, 0594/5/407—8,
0594/6/409—12
FAIREY VAP 6742/1044

0595 SU 09 NE Area centred SU 054953
ASHTON KEYNES, WILTSHIRE
Rectangular enclosures, trackways and ring ditches.
Cropmarks plotted by Dr. I.F. Smith in 1971.
CUAP AYG 39
NMR SU 0595/4/414—17
OS VAP 70/042/144

0694 SU 09 SE Area centred SU 069949
ASHTON KEYNES, WILTSHIRE
Linear features showing as soil marks.
OS VAP 70/030/124

0697 SU 09 NE Area centred SU 063979
SOUTH CERNEY, GLOUCESTERSHIRE
Trackway, enclosures and ring ditch, undated.
RCHM, South Cerney (3)
CUAP OAP AYG 40—1
NMR OAP SU 0697/5

MAP 3

0794 SU 09 SE SU 076946
ASHTON KEYNES, WILTSHIRE
Small enclosures and ring ditch, undated.
Cropmarks plotted by Dr. I.F. Smith in 1971.
OS VAP 70/030/123—4

0796 SU 09 NE Area centred SU 077968
LATTON, WILTSHIRE
Linear features and ring ditch, undated.
WALTERS VAP

0798 SU 09 NE Area centred on SU 072987
DRIFFIELD, GLOUCESTERSHIRE
Enclosures and linear ditches, undated. Of two
conjoined enclosures with entrances on the W, the
larger, covering about one third of a hectare, retains
traces of internal ditches semicircular on plan.
RCHM, Driffield (3)
NMR OAP SU 0798/1/259−60, 0798/2

0895 SU 09 NE Area centred SU 085958
LATTON, WILTSHIRE
Rectangular enclosures, trackways, ring ditch and
linear features, undated (plate 2).
WALTERS VAP

0896 SU 09 NE SU 08189680
LATTON, WILTSHIRE
Ring ditch, undated.
WILTS VAP 17/219085

0897 SU 09 NE SU 083975
LATTON, WILTSHIRE
Rectangular enclosure with sub-divisions, undated.
Grinsell 1957, 266
WILTS VAP 17/219087

0898 SU 09 NE SU 08859804
LATTON, WILTSHIRE
Romano-British burial.
Grinsell 1957, 80

0994 SU 09 NE SU 09709596
LATTON, WILTSHIRE
Rectangular enclosure.
Grinsell 1957, 266
WILTS VAP 18/219013

0995 SU 09 NE Area centred SU 095954
LATTON, WILTSHIRE
Trackway running from Ermine Street to enclosures of
Romano-British date and probable site of villa. Ring
ditches and oval enclosure to S of trackway. Enclosures
N and S of trackway (plate 3).
WALTERS VAP
CRAAGS OAP SU 0995/A−D (J.E. Hancock)
STONE OAP including colour transparency

0995 SU 09 NE SU 09929545
LATTON, WILTSHIRE
Romano-British building.
Wilts CC SU/09/NE/12

0995 SU 09 NE Area SU 098952
LATTON, WILTSHIRE
Group of three round barrows.
Grinsell 1957, 180

0997 SU 09 NE SU 091972
LATTON, WILTSHIRE
Enclosures and linear features, undated (plate 5).
Grinsell 1957, 266
NMR OAP SU 0997/9/103 transparencies

1094 SU 19 SW SU 100945
CRICKLADE and LATTON, WILTSHIRE
Probable Romano-British settlement
Grinsell 1957, 61

1094 SU 19 SW Area centred SU 103941
CRICKLADE, WILTSHIRE
Romano-British settlement.
Grinsell 1957, 61

1094 SU 19 SW Area centred SU 105949
LATTON, WILTSHIRE
Five converging roads, probably Roman, with
linear features and parchmarks of several rectangular
buildings to W. One road points towards the Romano-
British settlement at Cricklade SU 104941; a second
towards Ermine Street at SU 098947; a third towards
the settlement centred at SU 107958; the fourth
terminates at the settlement centred at SU 124953 and
the fifth runs for an unknown distance in a SE direction.
There are at least two phases to the pattern of the
road junction at ST 105949.
NMR SU 1094/5/65
STONE OAP including colour transparencies

1095/1096 SU 19 NW Area centred SU 102960
DOWN AMPNEY, GLOUCESTERSHIRE
Enclosures and linear ditches, undated. A sub-circular
enclosure 90 m in diameter, defined by an interrupted
ditch, is intersected by a straight ditch, possibly the
SE side of a rectilinear enclosure with an entrance on
the E. A small irregular oval enclosure in the E corner
of the rectilinear enclosure has a gap on the S side.
RCHM, Down Ampney (1)
NMR OAP SU 1095/6/327−8

1095/1096 SU 19 NW Area centred SU 108959
DOWN AMPNEY, GLOUCESTERSHIRE
Settlement and road covering about 4 acres, undated.
Twelve or more sub-rectangular and D-shaped enclosures
are partly surrounded by a ditch. Adjacent to the NE
are three or four rectangular plots each 15 m wide and
some 90 m long. The road is defined by two pairs of
side ditches each 12 m apart and of slightly differing
widths indicating reconstruction.
RCHM, Down Ampney (2)
NMR OAP SU 1096/1/325−6, 1095/7−8, 1095/10
(infra-red)

1096 SU 19 NW Area centred SU 10809665
DOWN AMPNEY, GLOUCESTERSHIRE
Rectangular enclosures, undated. An enclosure 60 m long
and 50 m wide is intersected almost at right angles by
ditches apparently belonging to another enclosure.
RCHM, Down Ampney (3)
NMR OAP SU 1096/3/305−7

Map 4. Cropmarks south of Fairford

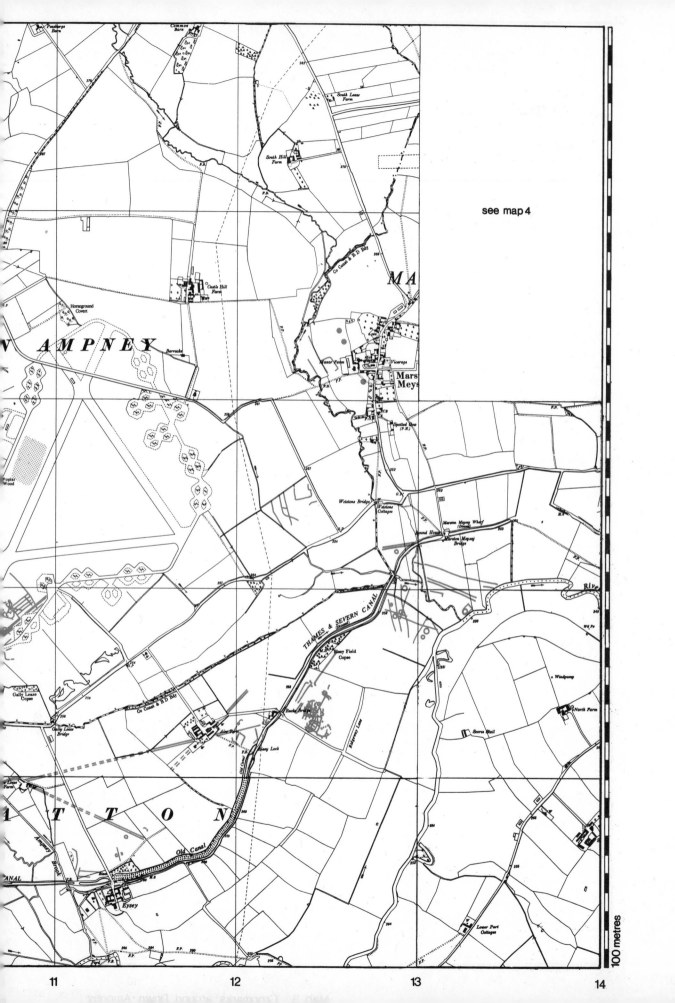

see map 4

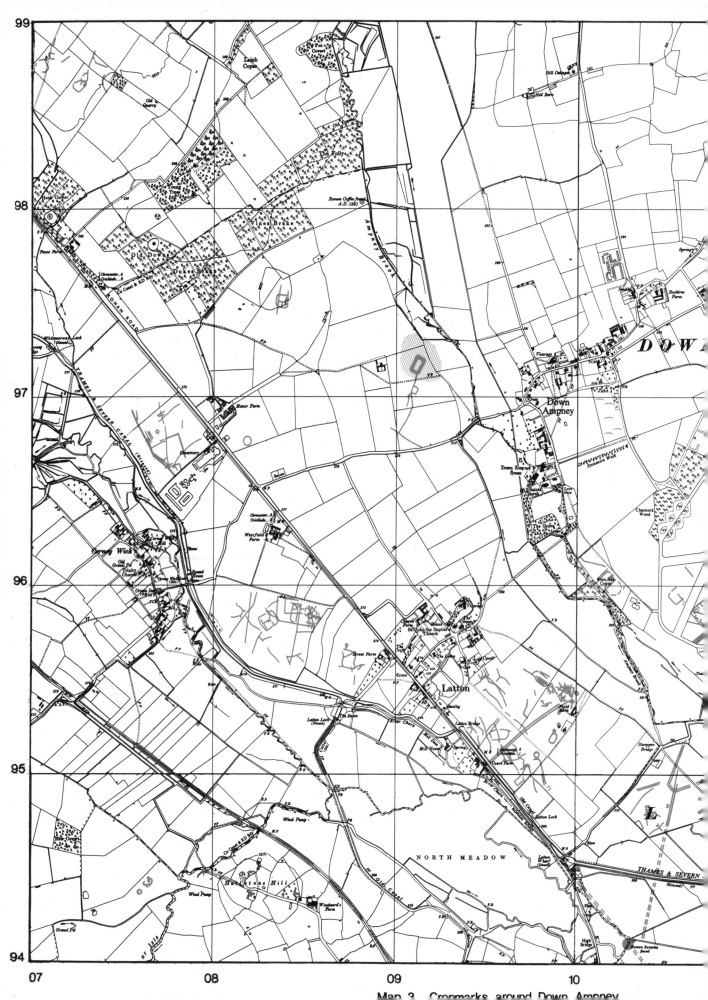

Map 3. Cropmarks around Down Ampney

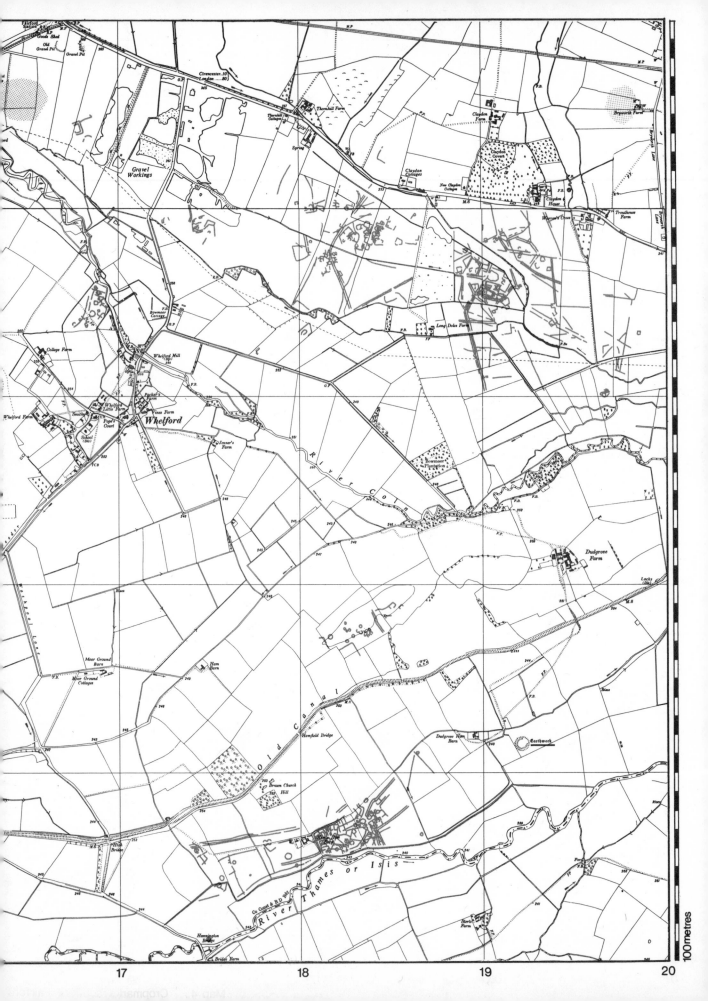

1194 SU 19 SW Area centred SU 113946
LATTON, WILTSHIRE
Linear features, penannular ditches and ring ditch,
undated.
STONE OAP colour transparencies

1195 SU 19 NW SU 118953
LATTON, WILTSHIRE
Junction of two roads, probably Romano-British. The
road pointing NE may join up with the road at SU
129963; for the road aligned WSE—ENE see 1094.
STONE OAP colour transparencies

1295 SU 19 NW SU 121952
LATTON, WILTSHIRE
Rectangular enclosure and linear features, undated.
STONE OAP colour transparency

1295 SU 19 NW Area centred SU 124953
LATTON, WILTSHIRE
Settlement consisting of probable Romano-British
rectangular enclosures with rounded corners, ring
ditches, many linear features and pits; the settlement is
approached by a road, from SU 105949, which does
not continue beyond to the E (plate 4).
STONE OAP colour transparencies

1295/1296/1395/1396 SU 19 NW Area centred
SU 129959
LATTON, WILTSHIRE
One penannular ditch, five ring ditches and linear features;
the five ring ditches are possibly the barrows noted by
Grinsell (1957, 180).
STONE OAP including colour transparency

1296 SU 19 NE Area centred SU 124965
DOWN AMPNEY, GLOUCESTERSHIRE
Rectilinear enclosure and linear features, undated.
RCHM, Down Ampney (4)
CUAP OAP BW 7

1297 SU 19 NW SU 12589736, 12609730
MARSTON MAISEY, WILTSHIRE
Two round barrows, W of village.
Grinsell 1957, 182

1297 SU 19 NW SU 12529720
MARSTON MAISEY, WILTSHIRE
Linear features visible as soil marks.
Grinsell 1957, 267
WILTS VAP 20/223070

1297 SU 19 NW SU 127971
MARSTON MAISEY, WILTSHIRE
Romano-British pottery.
WILTS CC SU/19/NW/6

MAP 4

1300 SP 10 SW Area centred SP 133003
FAIRFORD, GLOUCESTERSHIRE
Track, notably wide, undated, NW of Lady Lamb's copse.
There are indications of a settlement to the NE and also
to the SW across the county boundary with Wiltshire.
RCHM, Fairford (1)
NMR OAP SP 1300/1/404—7

1498/1499 SU 19 NW Area centred SU 141991
KEMPSFORD, GLOUCESTERSHIRE
Enclosures, tracks, ring ditch and linear ditches, undated,
covering some 7 hectares NW of Rhymes Barn.
RCHM, Kempsford (2)
NMR OAP SU 1499/2/409—11, 1499/3

1500 SP 10 SE SP 150005
KEMPSFORD, GLOUCESTERSHIRE
Romano-British settlement.
RCHM, Kempsford (1)

1596 SU 19 NE SU 15689631/15689629
CASTLE EATON, WILTSHIRE
Two round barrows.
Grinsell 1957, 164

1597 SU 19 NE SU 155975
KEMPSFORD, GLOUCESTERSHIRE
Ring ditch.
Riley 1942, 111 (Site 3)

1597/1697 SU 19 NE Area centred at SU 161974
KEMPSFORD, GLOUCESTERSHIRE
Enclosures and linear ditches extending over about 12
hectares N of the village.
RCHM, Kempsford (3)
NMR OAP SU 1597/1/418—2

1600 SP 10 SE Area centred SP 168004
FAIRFORD, GLOUCESTERSHIRE
Double-ditched enclosure of about one tenth of a hectare,
undated, partly disclosed by cropmarks on gravel N of
the R. Coln.
RCHM, Fairford (3)
CUAP OAP AM 32

1600 SP 10 SE Area centred SP 165005
FAIRFORD, GLOUCESTERSHIRE
Indistinct cropmarks over several hectares.
WILTS VAP 1800—1

1699 SU 19 NE Area centred at SU 168995
KEMPSFORD, GLOUCESTERSHIRE
Enclosures and linear ditches, undated, extending over
2 hectares on the W bank of the R. Coln. NW of Whelford.
RCHM, Kempsford (4)
ALLEN OAP 1368

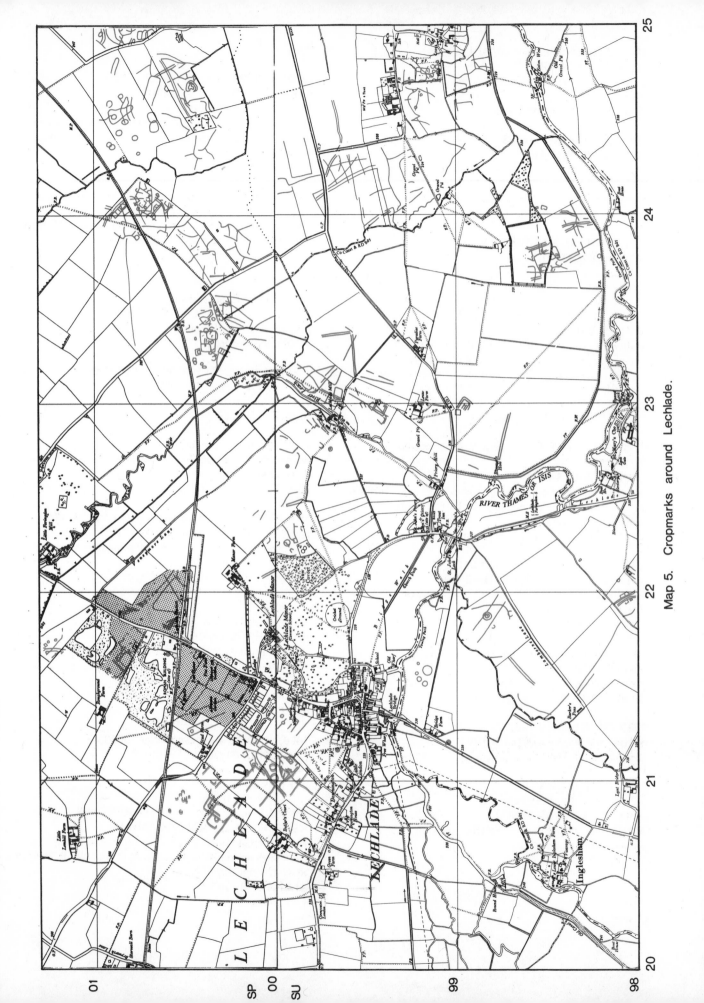

Map 5. Cropmarks around Lechlade.

1796/1896/1897 SU 19 NE Area centred at SU 180966
KEMPSFORD, GLOUCESTERSHIRE
Enclosures, tracks and linear ditches, undated, are
revealed by cropmarks extending over some 30 hectares
along the N bank of the Thames around Manor Ham
Barn. One of the focal points of the settlement complex
appears to be an 'open space' around a ring-ditch
(SU 18359672); there are only feint signs of other
ditches encroaching on its SW side (Frontispiece).
RCHM, Kempsford (7)
NMR SU 1896/8/423−32, 1896/9/426−7, 1896/11

1796 SU 19 NE SU 174961
KEMPSFORD, GLOUCESTERSHIRE
Romano-British debris.
OS/SU/19/NE/9

1799 SU 19 NE Area centred at SU 175999
FAIRFORD, GLOUCESTERSHIRE
Settlement with enclosures and tracks, undated. Site
first noted by Riley in 1943.
RCHM, Fairford (4)
CUAP VAP RC 8−M, 272−5; OAP CD 051, AXP 61,
AY1 6, 13

1800/1899/1900/1999 SP 10 SE/SU 19 NE
Area centred SU 183998, SU 191996
FAIRFORD and LECHLADE, GLOUCESTERSHIRE
Enclosures, tracks and linear ditches, undated, extending
over some 120 hectares (plate 1).
RCHM, Fairford (5−6) Lechlade (8)
CUAP VAP RC 8−M 272−5; OAP CD 051, VM 13−15,
AXP 61, 13, 68

1897 SU 19 NE Area centred at SU 184978
KEMPSFORD, GLOUCESTERSHIRE
Enclosures, undated, include small circular, penannular
and D-shaped features, WSW of Dudgrove Farm; cropmarks
extend over about 7 hectares on a low hill. Site first noted
by Riley in 1943.
RCHM, Kempsford (6)
CUAP OAP LY 86−7, AYI 2−3

1900 SP 10 SE Area centred SP 198006
LECHLADE, GLOUCESTERSHIRE
Linear ditches, undated, W of Bryworth Farm.
RCHM, Lechlade (14)
CUAP OAP DX 31

MAP 5

Cropmarks in Oxfordshire have already been published
(Benson & Miles 1974, 27−30); they are shown on Map 5
but are not mentioned in the Gazetteer.

2000/2099/2100/2199 SP 20 SW/SU 29 NW
Area centred SP 21102
LECHLADE, GLOUCESTERSHIRE
Enclosures, tracks, ring ditches and one double ring ditch,
undated, are revealed by cropmarks extending over some
20 hectares NW of the parish church. The SE ditch of
the track intersecting a ring-ditch at SP 209000 was almost
certainly cut into a mound within the ring-ditch. Triple
concentric circle, innermost with opening.
RCHM, Lechlade (2)
ALLEN OAP 721−2
CUAP OAP AM 29−30, CD 46−9, DX 32−4, PV 38−9,
VM 6−12, AFV 23, AYG 52, 54−7, 59, 61, AY1 20

2100 SP 20 SW Area centred SP 212004
LECHLADE, GLOUCESTERSHIRE
Cursus (50 m wide), first noted by D.N. Riley in 1942.
CUAP 62 AFV 19, 20, 22

2100/2200 SP 20 SW Area centred SP 217008
LECHLADE, GLOUCESTERSHIRE
Iron Age and Romano-British settlement, by
Roughground Farm, partly excavated before
destruction by gravel digging, extended over more
than 8 hectares W of the R. Leach and N of the
village. Excavations were carried out by Mrs. M.U.
Jones on behalf of the Ministry of Works from
1958 to 1965 (plate 7).
RCHM, Lechlade (5)
Ministry of Public Building and Works 1962, 8
Ministry of Public Building and Works 1963, 7
Ministry of Public Building and Works 1966, 5
CUAP OAP VQ 21, 31, 39, 40
NMR OAP (BAKER) 1994, 1997, 1998, 2006, 2010

2101 SP 20 SW Area centred SP 217013
LECHLADE, GLOUCESTERSHIRE
Ring ditches and probable settlement, undated, revealed
as small sub-circular and D-shaped enclosures and linear
ditches, covering about 1·5 hectares.
RCHM, Lechlade (6)
CUAP OAP VO 33

2199 SU NW Area centred SU 21589918
INGLESHAM, WILTSHIRE
Ring ditches.
WILTS CC SU/29/NW/3
WILTS VAP 24/227082

2199 SU 29 NW SU 21219905
INGLESHAM, WILTSHIRE
Romano-British pottery found.
WILTS CC SU/29/NW/2

2199 SU 29 NW SU 212996
LECHLADE, GLOUCESTERSHIRE
Iron Age pit excavated 1965.
RCHM, Lechlade (1)
Ministry of Public Building and Works 1966, 4

2298 SU 29 NW Area centred SU 228989
LECHLADE, GLOUCESTERSHIRE
Enclosure and tracks, undated, showing as cropmarks
E of the Thames and S of Leaze Farm.
RCHM, Lechlade (10)
NMR OAP SU 2298/1/385—6, 2298/3/438—9

2299 SU 29 NW Area centred SU 223999
LECHLADE, GLOUCESTERSHIRE
Enclosures, linear ditches and track, undated, extending
over about 2 hectares NE of the church.
RCHM, Lechlade (3)
NMR OAP SU 2299/3/383—4
CUAP OAP ZH 90
OS VAP 70/167/080—1

2299 SU 29 NW Area centred SU 277998
LECHLADE, GLOUCESTERSHIRE
Enclosures, round barrow, ring ditches, one double
ring-ditch and linear ditches, undated, extending over
about 8 hectares W of the R. Leach at Lechlade Mill.
RCHM, Lechlade (12)
Smith 1972, 160
ALLEN OAP 724
NMR OAP V 7—8 (D.N. Riley)
CUAP OAP ZH 91—2

2299/2399 SU 29 NW Area centred SU 228989
LECHLADE, GLOUCESTERSHIRE
Enclosure, tracks and linear ditches, undated, extending
over about 10 hectares E of the R. Leach at Lechlade
Mill. The enclosure occupies about one quarter of a
hectare.
RCHM, Lechlade (11)
ALLEN OAP 724
NMR OAP V 7—8 (D.N. Riley)
CUAP OAP ZH 91

2398/2498 SU 29 NW Area centred SU 238984
LECHLADE, GLOUCESTERSHIRE
Romano-British settlement, ploughed out, lies N of the
Thames and SE of Paradise Farm. Enclosures, tracks,
linear ditches and ring ditches cover some 9·5 hectares.
Romano-British pottery and limestone slabs indicate the
probable site of a building on slightly higher ground at
the N limit of the cropmarks (plate 8)
RCHM, Lechlade (13)
NMR OAP SU 2398/2/480—2, 2398/3/477—9

MAP 6

1695 SU 19 NE Area centred SU 165956
CASTLE EATON, WILTSHIRE
Three ring ditches (one with a central pit), linear
features and trackways at Blackford Farm. The trackway
are earlier than a pattern of ridge and furrow, which
showed also as cropmarks, but is not marked on the
map (plate 6).
STONE OAP including colour transparencies

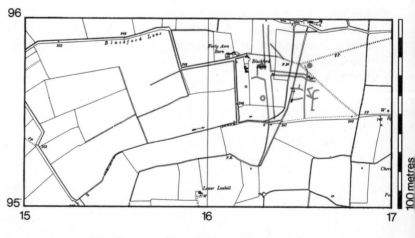

Map 6.   Cropmarks south of Kempsford

Plate 1   Cropmarks of settlements between Fairford and Lechlade. (Cambridge University Collections: copyright reserved)

Plate 2   Cropmarks at Street, Latton. (B. Walters: copyright reserved)

Plate 3   Cropmarks of a Romano-British settlement at Field Barn, Latton. (M. Stone: copyright reserved)

Plate 5   Cropmarks of rectangular enclosures north of Latton. (N.M.R. Air Photograph: crown copyright)

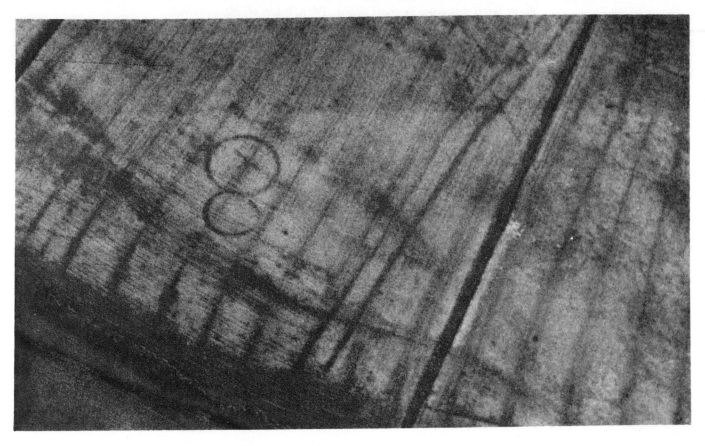

Plate 6   Cropmarks of ring-ditches and ridge and furrow near Castle Eaton. (M. Stone: copyright reserved)

Plate 7   Excavations in 1961 of the Iron Age and Romano-British settlement at Roughground Farm, Lechlade,
shortly before destruction by gravel digging. (W. A. Baker: copyright reserved)

Plate 8   Cropmarks of a Romano-British settlement at Paradise Farm, Lechlade. (N.M.R. Air Photograph: crown copyright)

6. DEVELOPMENT FACTORS AFFECTING ARCHAEOLOGICAL SITES

Gravel Extraction

6.1 In 1969 the Cotswold Water Park Joint Committee outlined past and future trends as follows:

'Production trends since 1950

The gravel pits of the Water Park lie within the Swindon Service Area. These Service Areas supply gravel principally to markets in Swindon and North Gloucestershire. Production from these Service Areas has increased from 0.3 million cubic metres (0.4 cubic yards) in 1950 to 1.5 million cubic metres (2 million cubic yards) in 1965. This was a faster growth rate than in the rest of the gravel region and the Service Areas' share of total production in the region rose from 20% to nearly 30% in the period.

Future Demand for Gravel

A review of sand and gravel production in south-east England was carried out by the Ministry of Housing and Local Government in 1967. This review made use of new forecasts published in 1965 by the Ministry of Public Building and Works. The main conclusion of the review was that by the middle 1970s the shortage of workable gravel fields in the London area will bring about a demand of gravel supplies from further afield. The Oxford and Swindon Service Areas were mentioned as being areas in which this additional demand might be met. The review does not give estimates of future demand and land requirements for individual Service Areas within the Middle and Upper Thames region.
However, there is every indication that the present rate of production in the Swindon Service Area will increase in the future, to meet further demand. . . . . . . The rate of gravel extraction must be related to the extent to which the road network within the Service Area can be developed to cope with the increased traffic. It is reasonable to assume an average annual rate of extraction for the period up to 1981 of 1.9 million cubic metres (2.5 million cubic yards) for the Swindon and Cotswold Service Areas. 23 million cubic metres (30 million cubic yards) or an additional 800 hectares (2,000 acres) will therefore be needed for working by 1981. The bulk of this will come from the Water Park area. Current Planning permissions to extract gravel cover about 600 hectares (1,500 acres), leaving 200 hectares (500 acres) of land which may have to be made available to meet the demand. Thus, there could be a total of about 1,200 hectares (3,000 acres) of wet pits by 1981.
Looking beyond 1981 to the end of the century, there is a possibility that the gravel reserves lying between the two main sections of the Water Park could also be worked, resulting in further areas of water forming a continuous series of lakes from Poole Keynes to Lechlade'.
(Cotswold Water Park Joint Committee 1969, 7–8)

6.2 The constraints envisaged in the 1969 report are not being strictly adhered to. Planning consents in the vicinity of Ashton Keynes have extended beyond the limits originally designated as 'gravel reserve areas'.

Suburban expansion

6.3 At present, the threat to archaeological sites posed by housing development is centred mainly on Cirencester and Lechlade. The discovery of new cropmark complexes in areas scheduled for development elsewhere could increase the number of threatened sites.
Part of the Neolithic cursus at Lechlade (Map 5: 2100) has been built over in the last two years, but the remainder, due to the foresight of Cotswold District Council, will be left as an open space reflecting the shape of the cursus in the middle of suburban housing. Settlement sites (Map 5: 2000) immediately south of the cursus are not likely to be built over for five years. North-east of Cirencester, enclosures and trackways of the early pre-Roman Iron Age at the Beeches (Map 1: 0301/0302), due to be covered by housing and a school within the next two years, were partly excavated by Dr. R.M. Reece in 1975 and 1976.

7. CASE STUDIES

7.1 Gravel extraction to date has been concentrated in two places: around Somerford Keynes and between Fairford and Lechlade. Extraction outside these areas is not likely to be permitted until the 1980s.

7.2. The following case studies outline the archaeological destruction which has already occurred in these two areas, the likely future destruction of the sites, and the history of the archaeological response.

CASE STUDY 1: AREA AROUND SOMERFORD KEYNES (Map 2, Fig. 4)

7.3 Gravel extraction in the Somerford Keynes area has taken place since the 1920s, but has increased greatly in the last ten years. Within the next ten to fifteen years over one quarter of the total land surface in the area covered by this map will be under water (Cotswold Water Park Joint Committee 1969). Several areas, apparently of archaeological importance, have already been totally or partly destroyed by gravel extraction.

Until 1971, knowledge of archaeological sites around Somerford Keynes came mainly from cropmarks and chance finds. The latter included a Palaeolithic hand axe, a Neolithic axe-head, Bronze Age metalwork and Romano-British material (Gingell 1971). The only detailed investigation undertaken was in 1971, when a site at Ashton Keynes (Map 2: 0294), which cropmarks had indicated was of later prehistoric or Romano-British date, was shown by excavation to belong entirely to the latter period (4.5; Map 2: 0294).

A Penny for your Past (Gingell 1971) emphasised the acute threat to certain sites in the Somerford Keynes area, but no further research has been undertaken to date. Two complexes, probably Iron Age and Romano-British enclosures, have now been partly destroyed without any archaeological investigation (Map 2: 0193, 0495). Fig. 4 shows that the majority of the surviving known archaeological sites lie within areas which have received planning consent for future gravel extraction.

The two most extensive and interesting cropmark sites now threatened are at Somerford Keynes (Map 2: 0396) and Ashton Keynes (Map 2: 0495). The former is likely to include enclosures of both Iron Age and Romano-British date. The latter, already partly destroyed, probably incorporates elements from the Bronze Age, Iron Age and Romano-British periods.

Within the three counties of Avon, Gloucestershire and Somerset, with the exception of the Glastonbury and Meare Lake Villages (Bulleid and Gray 1911: 1917; 1948, Gray and Bulleid 1953; Gray and Cotton 1966; Avery 1968; Tratman 1970), no undefended settlement of Iron Age date has been totally, or even half, excavated. Excavations at Tollard Royal, Wiltshire (Wainwright 1968) and Gussage All Saints, Dorset (Wainwright and Spratling 1973) have shown the value of large-scale exploration on this type of site. For the Romano-British period research has concentrated almost exclusively on military sites, towns and villas. The only rural settlements excavated in detail have been Butcombe (Fowler 1970), Camerton (Wedlake 1958), Catsgore (Leech 1973), and the sites at Ashton Keynes and Lechlade already referred to (4.5, 7.3).

If a true understanding is to be obtained of the Iron Age and Romano-British landscape in the Cotswold and Upper Thames Valley, large-scale excavations of rural settlements and their associated features must be undertaken. The importance of examining settlements of this type has been emphasised elsewhere:

> 'practically nothing is know of the apparently nucleated settlements, often associated with trackways, which are now particularly well represented in the western part of the valley' (Benson & Miles 1974, 100).

There is thus a strong case for examining some of the threatened sites referred to above. This could probably best be achieved by a carefully formulated programme of investigation over several years.

CASE STUDY 2: AREA SOUTH OF FAIRFORD (Map 4; Fig. 5)

7.4 No archaeological investigations have taken place in the area between Fairford and Lechlade, and current knowledge has mainly been derived from cropmarks and chance finds. The latter include Bronze Age metalwork, Romano-British material and an Anglo-Saxon burial with bronze hanging bowl and beads (Gingell 1971).

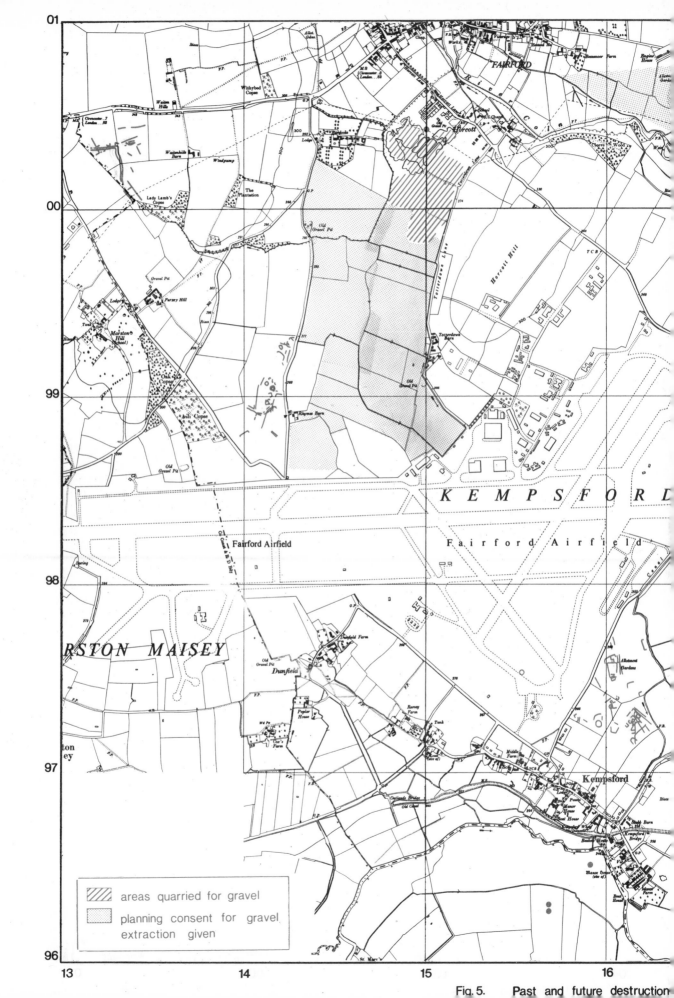

areas quarried for gravel

planning consent for gravel
extraction given

Fig. 5.   Past and future destruction

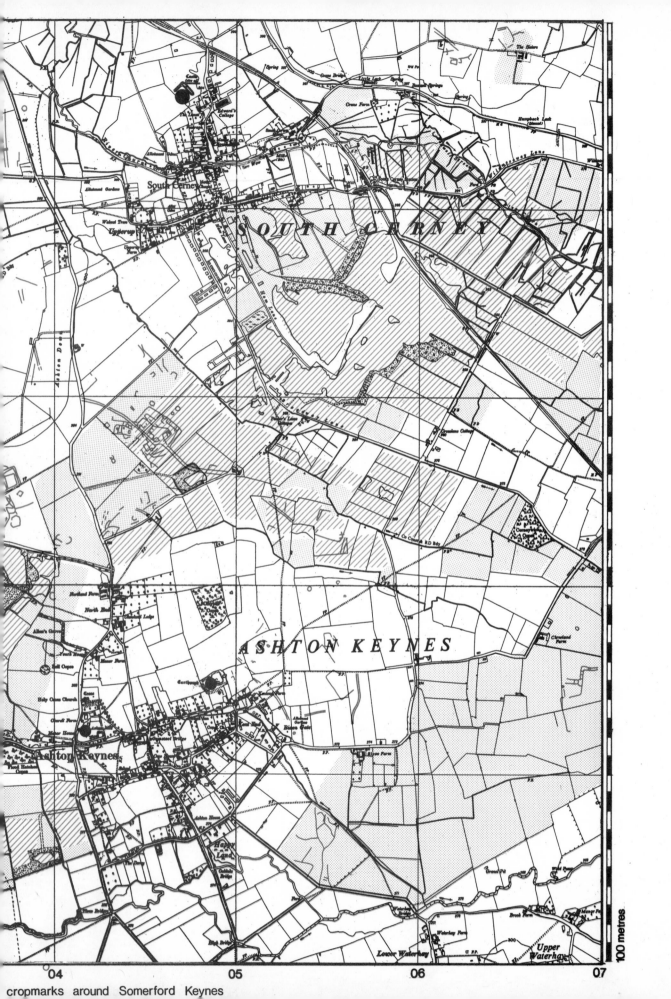

cropmarks around Somerford Keynes

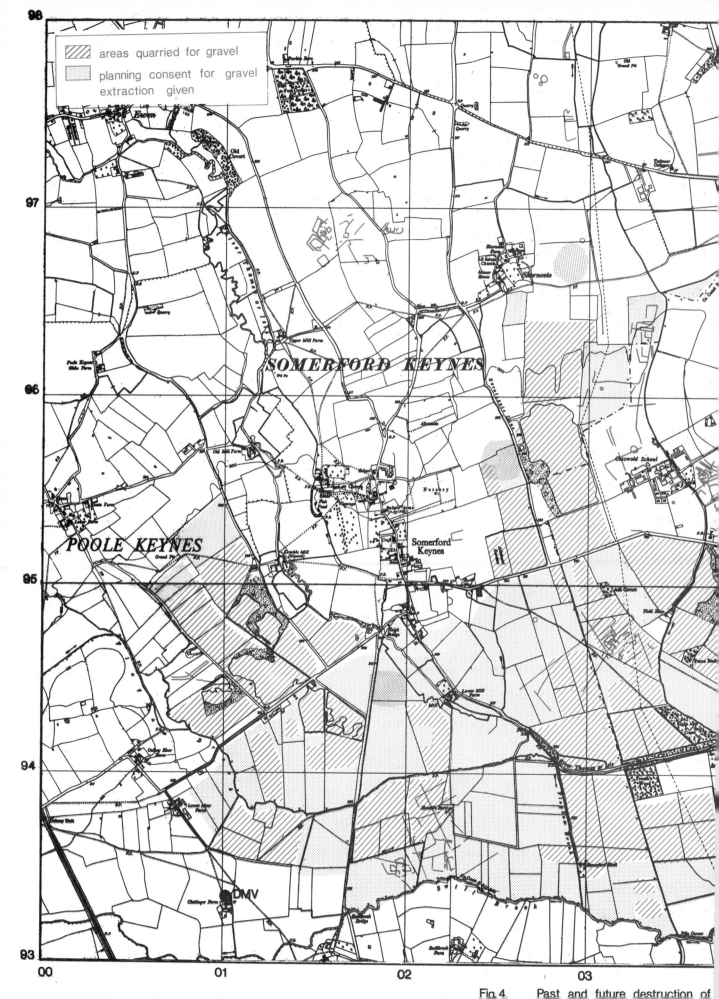

areas quarried for gravel

planning consent for gravel
extraction given

SOMERFORD KEYNES

POOLE KEYNES

Somerford
Keynes

DMV

Fig. 4.   Past and future destruction of

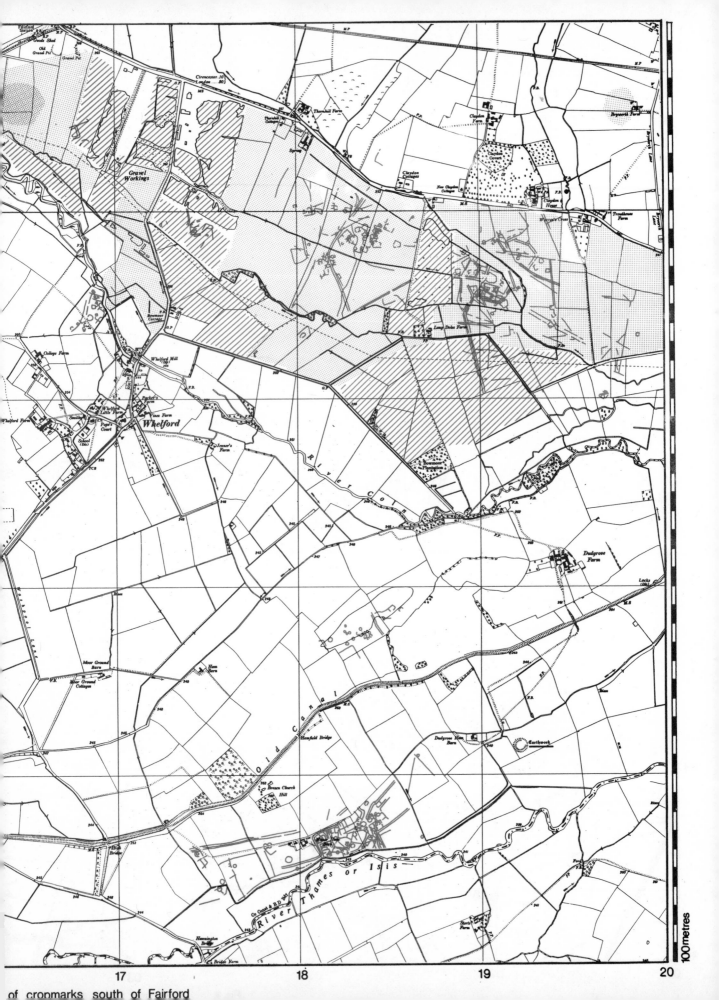

Planning consents already given for gravel extraction and the proposals outlined in 1969 (Cotswold Water Park Joint Committee 1969) make it clear that the entire area north of the River Coln between Fairford and Lechlade will become a contiguous series of lakes. Furthermore, the area between the Coln and the Thames is not entirely safe from gravel extraction. In 1971 the *Plan for the River Thames: Lechlade to Cricklade* stated that 'should eventually it be found feasible to connect the Claydon Lakes section of the proposed Cotswold Water Park to the Thames by lock . . . the gravel bearing land could be excavated to form a series of small cruising lakes interconnected by channels' (Gloucesterhsire and Wiltshire County Councils 1971, 11).

The lakes already conceived (i.e. areas with existing planning consent for gravel extraction) will destroy the largest known complex of cropmarks in the Gloucestershire-Wiltshire section of the Upper Thames Valley (P1.1; Map 4: 1800). The cropmarks, which are mainly intact, are of several distinct nucleated settlements with numerous associated trackways and enclosures spreading over 120 hectares. Many of the features are likely to be of Iron Age or Romano-British date. Only a small part of the area has already been destroyed and an opportunity exists here to examine a settlement complex of a type not extensively excavated before in southern England. In certain areas total excavation is likely to be necessary, mainly where cropmarks indicate groups of buildings. Selective excavation over a much wider area will reveal information about the development of field boundaries, trackways, cemeteries and other features.

Gravel extraction in the area south of Fairford is likely to continue for about twenty years. Excavation and publication should be structured to take place during this period.

8. ARCHAEOLOGICAL PROVISION

8.1. In many parts of the country funds provided by the Department of the Environment for recording archaeological sites prior to destruction are now being administered through Regional or County organisations. This is the case with both Gloucesterhsire and Wiltshire, although archaeological provision in the two counties is very different and must be considered separately.

Committee for Rescue Archaeology in Avon, Gloucestershire and Somerset

8.2 In Gloucestershire, Department of the Environment funds for rescue archaeology are now administered by the Committee for Rescue Archaeology in Avon, Gloucestershire and Somerset (CRAAGS is a sub-committe of the Council for British Archaeology, Regional Group 13) to ensure that decisions on expenditure are reached within an academically justifiable and publicly understood framework of archaeological research.

8.3 In certain parts of the region where no continuing archaeological provision existed prior to 1974, CRAAGS has undertaken rescue projects to fill the gaps, and at the same time working towards an overall policy for the three counties. These projects are staffed by a permanent excavation team and include a programme of investigation on threatened areas in the medieval towns of Somerset. CRAAGS has also instigated and is publishing surveys of 'archaeological potential' such a Small Medieval Towns in Avon (Leech 1975), this report on the Upper Thames Valley in Gloucestershire and Wiltshire, and a forthcoming survey of medieval towns in Gloucestershire, which will include Fairford and Lechlade.

Corinium Museum, Cirencester

8.4 Since local government reorganisation, Corinium Museum has been administered by Cotswold District Council, which includes within its area the Gloucestershire section of the Cotswold Water Park. The Museum has recently been more than doubled in size. Although the academic staff at present consists of only a Curator and an Assistant, it is hoped that there will be further appointments in the future to cope with the archaeological needs throughout Cotswold District. The museum has already begun work on the preparation of an archaeological Sites and Monuments Record for the District.

Wiltshire County Council: Libraries and Museums Service

8.5   The Libraries and Museums Service of Wiltshire County Council maintains a Sites and Monuments Record for the County and works in liaison with the County and District Planning Offices on archaeological matters. The Service is not at present able to carry out large-scale excavations of threatened sites but it does organise watching briefs and small excavations.

Wiltshire Archaeological and Natural History Society

8.6   In Wiltshire, the Archaeological Research Committee of the County Archaeological Society works with the Department of the Environment on the execution of a rescue archaeology programme, now aided by two field officers. This Committee includes representatives of all archaeological institutions and societies in the county.

Conservation

8.7   Full laboratory facilities for the treatment and storage of archaeological material exist at Trowbridge, in the Wiltshire County Council Libraries and Museums Service. Corinium Museum, Cirencester, has a large amount of space allocated for conservation work, but no staff have yet been appointed.

Local Societies

8.8   In Gloucestershire there is no local amateur archaeological society working within the area of the Upper Thames Valley. In Wiltshire, the Swindon Archaeological Society has undertaken much valuable fieldwork and excavation. Through the University of Bristol Department of Extra-Mural Studies, CBA Regional Groups 12 and 13 publish the Archaeological Review annually. This carries short articles and up-to-date information on fieldwork and excavation. The Upper Thames Valley falls within the area covered by two county societies, both of which publish annual journals: the Wiltshire Archaeological and Natural History Society (Wiltshire Archaeological Magazine) and the Bristol and Gloucestershire Archaeological Society (Transactions of the Bristol and Gloucestershire Archaeological Society).

National Organisations

8.9   The resources and functions of a number of national bodies are relevant to work in the Upper Thames region.

a)   Directorate of Ancient Monuments and Historic Buildings. Government funds for rescue excavation are channelled through this department. The Ancient Monuments Board and its inspectors are responsible for the administration of the Ancient Monuments Acts.

b)   The Royal Commission on Historical Monuments (including the National Monuments Record, Air Photography Unit). Its publication in 1960 of *A Matter of Time* drew attention to the problems of gravel sites generally and the Commission's forthcoming volume on Gloucestershire will provide a valuable source of information for gravel sites of the Iron Age and Romano-British periods in the area. Although its resources are limited the National Monuments Record, Air Photography Unit, maintains an invaluable and efficiently organised collection of aerial photographs which performs an essential role in the provision of a central archive for aerial photographs.

c)   Ordnance Survey (Archaeology Division). The Division houses a topographical archive of outstanding value and the work of its investigators provides a resource for the recording of field monuments, a task which frequently cannot be undertaken locally.

d)   A large number of aerial photographs, from diverse sources, are now housed within the National Monuments Record. The well-known collection of Professor St. Joseph's photographs is maintained at Cambridge University (Committee for Aerial Photography).

9. ARCHAEOLOGY, LEGISLATION AND PLANNING

9.1   A detailed account of this subject appeared in the report on the Upper Thames Valley in Oxfordshire (Benson and Miles 1974).

9.2   The situation in Gloucestershire may be summarised by saying that for various reasons neither the Gloucestershire County Council nor Cotswold District Council have been able to implement the recommendations of Circular 11/72 (Field Monuments and Local Authorities):

RECOMMENDATIONS OF THE FIELD MONUMENTS COMMITTEE DIRECTED AT LOCAL AUTHORITIES

Paragraph 50

The safeguarding of unscheduled field monuments is a matter for local authorities to consider through the use of their planning powers and otherwise.

Paragraph 70

Local authorities should take more field monuments into guardianship.

Paragraphs 77–78

County planning authorities should maintain a consolidated record of known field monuments.

Paragraph 82

Local Land Charge Registries should ensure that scheduling notices are so registered that a properly conducted search will reveal them.

Paragraph 95

Local planning authorities could attach suitable conditions for planning permissions for mineral extraction.

Paragraph 111

Local authorities should consider the protection of the amenities of outstanding field monuments.

Paragraph 115

Local authorities should make arrangements for improved publicity at a local level.

Paragraph 150

Local authorities should increase their interest and efforts generally in relation to field monuments.

Paragraph 152

Local authorities should consider arrangements for regular inspection of the more important unscheduled field monuments in their areas.

Paragraph 155

County Councils with many field monuments in their areas may find it helpful to foster the establishment of informal liaison committees to enhance co-operation between archaeologists and farmers/foresters and other land operators such as gravel extractors or other mineral operators whose activities are a potential threat to field monuments.

Paragraphs 158–161

County Councils should consider appointing archaeological officers either individually or, in appropriate cases, on a shared or part-time basis. These officers should maintain close relations with the planning department and keep in close touch with the Department's Inspectorate of Ancient Monuments.

9.3   In Wiltshire, these recommendations have been partly fulfilled by the appointment of an Archaeological Officer with supporting staff in the Libraries and Museums Service.

9.4   In the adjacent counties of Hereford, Worcester, Warwickshire and Oxfordshire, Archaeological Officers have been placed in the respective County Libraries and Museums Services. Somerset has appointed an Archaeologist in the Conservation Section of the County Council's Planning Department.

9.5   The absence of archaeological advice to the relevant Planning Offices was well illustrated in the *Plan for the River Thames: Lechlade to Cricklade* (Gloucestershire and Wiltshire County Councils 1971). This document contained a list which included 'many of the potential places of archaeological, historic and architectural interest'. The archaeological sites were confined to Scheduled Ancient Monuments alone, and consequently omitted the considerable information about many unscheduled field monuments of local importance which could have been supplied by the Ordnance Survey Archaeology Division and the Royal Commission on Historical Monuments. Even the nationally important earthworks of the Anglo-Saxon burh at Cricklade received no mention.

10. ARCHAEOLOGICAL PROBLEMS AND POTENTIAL

General problems

10.1   In recent years, intensive archaeological fieldwork in many parts of the country has shown that previous estimates of site numbers and densities may be multiplied several times. In the Gloucestershire and Wiltshire parts of the Upper Thames Valley there has been little field-work and only a limited air photographic coverage. Detailed fieldwork linked to a programme of intense aerial photography could considerably increase the number of sites known (3.3), and contribute significantly to a fuller understanding of the whole landscape.

10.2   By c. AD 2000 the continued extraction of gravel in the Water Park will result in the destruction of an additional area substantially larger than that already destroyed. Since it is virtually certain that there are many more sites awaiting discovery in the threatened areas (3.3), a succession of buried or relict landscapes will be totally destroyed.

10.3   The potential for studying successive historic landscapes is considerable, but as yet almost nothing is known of the ways in which settlements developed. The intensity of cropmarks often illustrates the pressures on land and the restrictions imposed by fields and barrows on settlement areas. Trackways linking settlements indicate the possibility of studying larger tracts of landscape; the importance of river communications in relation to trackways and settlements has not been studied at all. Fuller air photographic coverage will also indicate areas which have never been settled and which are devoid of sites (as evidenced by cropmarks).

Problems relating to particular periods

10.4   The scarcity of Neolithic and Bronze Age settlement sites before c. 1000 BC compared to the distribution of funerary and religious monuments of the same period has been noted elsewhere (Benson and Miles 1974, 99–100). In the Cotswold Water Park area no Neolithic long barrows have been identified and the cursus at Lechlade (Map 5: 2100) lies in contemporary isolation.

10.5   Round barrows of the second millenium BC are much more numerous, and have been closely studied (O'Neill and Grinsell 1960; Smith 1972). The ways in which later features, particularly trackways, take note of, or ignore, earlier barrows is of great interest (Map 4: 1796/1896/1897; Map 5 2000/2099/2100/2199). Settlements of this period have not yet been identified, although they may already exist as cropmarks.

10.6   Research into rural settlements of the Iron Age and Romano-British periods have been confined to the excavations carried out at Lechalde and Ashton Keynes (4.5). In contrast, much research has been carried out on Iron Age hillforts and *oppida* such as Crickley Hill (Dixon 1973) and Bagendon (Clifford 1961), on the Roman town of Cirencester (4.7), and on numerous villas such as Barnsley Park (Webster 1967), Chedworth (Richmond 1959) and Whittington (O'Neill 1952). The opportunities for studying complete landscapes of these periods in the vicinity of Somerford Keynes and Fairford have already been outlined (7.3, 7.4); the outstanding complex of settlements and roads in the Latton area should be preserved for future generations to study.

10.7   Very little is known of the archaeology of the region in the fifth to seventh centuries AD. Research has shown the importance of finds which may be indicative of the presence of Germanic soldiers and settlers in the Upper Thames Valley in the later fourth and fifth centuries (Hawkes and Dunning 1961), but no contemporary settlement sites have been identified comparable to those recognised in the Oxford region.

10.8   As mentioned above (1.6), to achieve conformity with the report on the Oxfordshire gravels (Benson and Miles 1974) no detailed assessment of the medieval period has been included. This is no less important than any other historical period and recent writers have emphasised the extent to which parts of the medieval landscape have survived as relict features to the present day:

> 'The present patchwork nature of settlement and patterns of agriculture has evolved as a result of thousands of years of human endeavour, producing a landscape which possesses not only a beauty associated with long and slow development, but an inexhaustible store of information about many kinds of human activity in the past.'

(Aston and Rowley 1974, 14)

10.9   In the area of the Cotswold Water Park there is an urgent need for extensive topographical studies of the medieval and later landscape. Extant, shrunken, migrated or deserted villages should be examined in detail, with emphasis on features such as the village plan, churchyards, the disposition of land parcels, greens and house platforms. Tracts of countryside around former medieval villages will include strip fields surviving as ridge and furrow or lynchets, moated farmsteads, fishponds, mill sites, roads and bridges, all of which would repay attention in detail. The sources for research will include not only fieldwork and documentary material, but also air photographs, often taken for purposes other than archaeology.

11.   PRESERVATION, SURVEY AND EXCAVATION

Preservation

11.1   In conditions of rapid destruction of archaeological landscapes, preservation must have a part in any overall policy. Some areas must be left for future research by archaeologists equipped with a far greater range of skills and techniques than are available now.

11.2   As part of the development of planning strategy, zones of high archaeological value should be taken into account. A form of grading is proposed here which may aid this process. It is a grading which takes account of the areas of destruction in the past and the likely pressures in the future (see Appendix)

Category 1:   Sites which should be preserved. These are chosen because of their completeness and extent; they are, in most cases, in areas unlikely to be immediately threatened by gravel extraction or other developments.

Category 2*:   Sites where preservation is highly desirable. Any development would need to be preceded by large-scale excavation.

Category 2:   Sites which are archaeologically important, but where it is felt that existing pressures make the possibilities of preservation unlikely. Excavation is however essential prior to development.

Category 3:   Areas subject to development; a watching brief should automatically be carried out and excavation may be necessary. Included here would be areas where no cropmarks are known, or where they are thinly scattered, or where advance excavation was judged to be of low archaeological priority. These are not listed in the Appendix.

Survey

11.3   A policy aimed at recovering the type of information mentioned above (10. 1–9) must include several elements. Apart from excavation (12. 3–7), fuller aerial coverage, together with repeated photography of selected cropmark complexes, are required. The plotting of cropmarks in more detail is a prerequisite of archaeological analysis; this needs to be supported by a programme of intensive surface fieldwork, not only on known cropmark sites, but over the county as a whole, perhaps on a parochial basis. Such a programme particularly lends itself to participation by voluntary groups.

Excavation

11.4   An excavation policy, too, needs to have several strands closely integrated within a wide framework of research and preservation. Large-scale area excavations should be conducted on major complexes, selected on academic grounds, with a full awareness of the whole range of sites available and, perforce, of the development plans affecting them. It would not be necessary to carry out the total excavation of large complexes at one time – indeed this would be impracticable – but a total record should be built up over a period of years, as opportunity dictates.

11.5   In other circumstances, watching briefs should be maintained, which may lead to selected salvage operations.

11.6   There is also an academic case for small-scale excavations on areas not necessarily threatened by quarrying, in order to illuminate problems encountered elsewhere. Such investigations may be necessary, for example, on the fringes of excavated complexes.

12. RECOMMENDATIONS

Legislation and Planning

12.1   The relevant County and District Councils should ensure that all aspects of the historical and archaeological environment are given adequate provision in planning. The recommendations of Circular 11/72 should be adopted wherever possible (9. 1—5).

12.2   The recommendations for sites to be preserved should be adopted (11.2, Appendix 1).

Archaeological Policy

12.3   A long term strategy must be adopted for gravel sites within the Cotswold Water Park. This should be aimed at the investigation and interpretation of whole landscapes, which may extend beyond the gravel terraces. The Fairford-Lechlade area, in particular, should be subjected to large-scale excavations (10.1—9).

12.4   The necessary programme of excavation and other research could be based on Corinium Museum, Cirencester, with an essential condition being the realistic support of the relevant County and District Councils. In recommending this, CRAAGS has taken into consideration the great potential that exists there for   the conservation and display of excavated material from archaeological sites investigated in the Water Park. Cotswold District is also one of the richest archaeological areas in the country and it would be entirely appropriate for Corinium Museum to assume enlarged responsibilities as the archaeological centre for a programme of excavation and recording on threatened sites in its locality (8.4, 8.7).

12.5   A comparatively small amount of research and rescue excavation is likely to take place on the Wiltshire gravels (7.3). This should be co-ordinated with work in Gloucestershire. Such a joint approach would be in keeping with the spirit of the Cotswold Water Park Joint Committee. In the case of excavations in Wiltshire it could be appropriate for the storage, conservation and display of excavated material to be the responsibility of the Libraries and Museums Service, Wiltshire County Council (8.5).

12.6   The implementation of the excavation programme should be carried out from 1977 onwards, following detailed discussions between CRAAGS and the Department of the Environment, the County Councils, Cotswold District Council and the Joint Committee. If it is found that certain threatened sites cannot be excavated due to lack of resources, these should be brought to the attention of other institutions, not funded by the Department of the Environment.

12.7   Further aerial survey is needed, which should be accompanied by the rapid dissemination of results (3.3, 10.1),

Conclusion

12.8   It is now three years since *A Penny for Your Past* outlined the great threat to archaeological sites in the Cotswold Water Park. Since then, gravel extraction has continued apace and a number of important sites have been destroyed. This report now demonstrates in greater detail the opportunities and the urgent need for archaeological research. It must be doubted whether the two counties can afford to contemplate the total destruction of so much evidence from such important an area without co-operating in efforts to record and display that evidence for the public benefit. With the establishment of the Committee for Rescue Archaeology in Avon, Gloucestershire and Somerset and with a greatly extended Corinium Museum, the means for taking action now exist. If the opportunity is not seized an important but unexplored part of Gloucestershire's and Wiltshire's heritage will have been lost for ever, in one generation.

APPENDIX

SITE GRADING AND PRESERVATION – A SUGGESTED GRADING OF CROPMARK SITES (OTHER SITES ARE NOT INCLUDED)

CATEGORY 1 Sites recommended for preservation

1. Map 1 SP 0100 SU 0199
   Cirencester-Siddington, Gloucestershire
   Extending over 15 hectares, includes Romano-British settlement.

2. Map 1 SP 0500
   Preston, Gloucestershire
   Enclosures and ditches, undated, W of St. Augustine's Farm.

3. Map 1 SP 0602
   Ampney Crucis, Gloucestershire
   Probable settlement over 12 hectares S of Akeman Street, mainly to N of Map 1.

4. Map 2 SU 0196
   Somerford Keynes, Gloucestershire
   Probable settlement extending over 10 hectares E and W of present road.

5. Map 2 SU 0395
   Ashton Keynes, Wiltshire
   Settlement with trackways and rectangular enclosures, one of only two complete surviving examples in this area.

6. Map 3 SU 0895
   Latton, Wiltshire
   Rectangular enclosures, trackways; probable settlement extending over 2 hectares.

7. Map 3 SU 0995
   Latton, Wiltshire
   Enclosures and trackways, probably associated with a Roman villa.

8. Map 3 SU 1095/1096
   Down Ampney, Gloucestershire
   Settlement and road covering 1.5 hectares, sub circular enclosure to NW.

9. Map 3 SU 1295
   Latton, Wiltshire
   Probable Romano-British settlement extending over 1.5 hectares.

10. Map 4 SU 1597/1697
    Kempsford, Gloucestershire
    Enclosures and linear ditches extending over 12 hectares.

11. Map 4 SU 1796/1896/1897
    Kempsford, Gloucestershire
    Enclosures, tracks and linear ditches extending over some 30 hectares. The largest complete unthreatened complex of cropmarks in the Water Park now surviving.

12. Map 5 SP 2200 SU 2299/2399
    Lechlade, Gloucestershire
    Enclosures, trackways, linear ditches, ring ditches, double ring ditch, E and W of River Leach.

13. Map 5 SU 2398
    Lechlade, Gloucestershire
    Romano-British settlement extending over 9 hectares.

CATEGORY 2* Preservation desirable — large-scale excavation essential if any form of development should take place.

1. Map 1 SP 0400 SU 0499
   Worms Farm, Siddington, Gloucestershire
   Romano-British settlement, partly sealed by buildings on South Cerney Airfield.

2. Map 1 SU 0599/0699
   Driffield, Gloucestershire
   Enclosures, linear ditches and ring ditch, undated.

3. Map 2 SU 0196
   Somerford Keynes, Gloucestershire
   Probable settlement, undated, over some 6.5 hectares. Includes double ditched enclosure.

4. Map 2 SU 0297
   Siddington, Gloucestershire
   Enclosure, trackway and ring ditches.

5. Map 2 SU 0594
   Ashton Keynes, Wiltshire
   Enclosures, linear features and ring ditches; includes small enclosure with possible buildings.

6. Map 2 SU 0697
   South Cerney, Gloucestershire
   Trackway, enclosures and ring ditches.

7. Map 3 SU 1094
   Latton, Wiltshire
   Junction of five Romano-British roads.

8. Map 3 SU 1295/1395
   Latton, Wiltshire
   Group of one penannular ditch and five ring ditches.

9. Map 4 SU 1699
   Kempsford, Gloucestershire
   Enclosures and linear ditches, extending over 2 hectares.

10, Map 4 SU 1897
   Kempsford, Gloucestershire
   Enclosures, including small circular, penannular and D-shaped features, extending over about 7 hectares.

CATEGORY 2 — Excavation essential prior to any future development

1. Map 1 SP 0301/0302
   The Beeches, Cirencester, Gloucestershire
   Enclosures and probable settlement over about 14 hectares.

2. Map 1 SP 0301
   Preston, Gloucestershire
   Linear features and enclosures over about 5 hectares, partly cut by Cirencester By-Pass.

3. Map 2 SU 0193/0293
   Somerford Keynes, Gloucestershire
   Probable settlement extending over 14 hectares. Destruction likely within 2–3 years.

4.   Map 2 SU 0396
     Somerford Keynes, Gloucestershire and Ashton Keynes, Wiltshire Settlement with trackways
     and at least 5 rectangular enclosures; part of the site already has planning consent for
     gravel extraction. One of only two surviving examples in this area.

5.   Map 2 SU 0495/0496
     Ashton Keynes, Wiltshire
     Settlement with rectangular and sub-rectangular enclosures, partly destroyed, remainder likely
     to disappear within 2–3 years.

6.   Map 4 SU 1498/1499
     Kempsford, Gloucestershire
     Enclosures, tracks, ring ditch and linear ditches.

7.   Map 4 SU 1800/1899/1900/1999
     Fairford and Lechlade, Gloucestershire
     Enclosures, tracks, linear ditches, extending over some *120 hectares* all likely to be destroyed
     by 1995.

8.   Map 5 SP 2000/2100 SU 2099/2199
     Lechlade, Gloucestershire
     Enclosures, tracks, ring ditches and one double ring ditch, extending over some 20 hectares.

REFERENCES

Aston, M. & Rowley, R.T., 1974.
Landscape Archaeology (Newton Abbot).

Avery, M., 1968.
'Excavations at Meare East, 1966, 1968', *Proc. Somerset Archaeol. Natur. Hist. Soc.* cxii, 21–39.

Benson, D. & Miles, D., 1974.
The Upper Thames Valley: An Archaeological Survey of the River Gravels (Oxford).

Bonney, D.J., 1973.
'The Pagan Saxon Period c. 500–700', *Victoria County History: Wiltshire* i, pt 2, 468–484.

Bulleid, A & Gray, H.St.G., 1911.
The Glastonbury Lake Village i (Glastonbury)

Bulleid, A. & Gray, H.St.G., 1917.
The Glastonbury Lake Village ii (Glastonbury).

Bullied, A. & Gray, H.St.G., 1948.
The Meare Lake Village i (Taunton).

Clifford, E.M., 1961.
Bagendon: a Belgic Oppidum. A Record of the Excavations of 1954–56 (Cambridge).

Cotswold Water Park Joint Committee, 1969.
Cotswold Water Park (Gloucester).

Cunliffe, B.W., 1973.
'The Early pre-Roman Iron Age . . . (to) . . . The End of the Romon Era', *Victoria County History: Wiltshire* i, pt 2, 408–467.

Department of the Environment, 1971.
Archaeological Excavations 1970 (London).

Department of the Environment, 1972.
Archaeological Excavations 1971 (London).

Department of the Environment, 1973.
Archaeological Excavations 1972 (London).

Department of the Environment, 1974.
Archaeological Excavations 1973 (London).

Dixon, P., 1973.
Crickley Hill, Fifth Report 1973 (privately printed).

Evans, J.G., 1972.
'Ice wedge casts at Broome Heath, Norfolk', *Proc. Prehist. Soc.* xxxviii, 77–86.

Fowler, P.J., 1970.
'Fieldwork: Excavation in the Butcombe Area, North Somerset: Second interim report', *Proc. Univ. Bristol Spelaeol. Soc.* xii, 169–94.

Gates, T., 1975
The Middle Thames Valley: An Archaeological Survey of the River Gravels (Oxford).

Gingell, C.J., undated.
A Penny for your Past: Archaeology and the Water Park (privately printed by the Committee for Research into the Iron Age in the North-West Cotswolds).

Gloucestershire & Wiltshire County Councils, 1971.
Plan for the River Thames: Lechlade to Cricklade (Gloucester).

Gray, H.St.G. & Bulleid, A., 1953.
The Meare Lake Village ii (Taunton).

Gray, H. St. G & Cotton, M.A. (eds.), 1966.	*The Meare Lake Village* iii (Taunton).
Grinsell, L.V., 1957.	'Archaeological Gazetteer', *Victoria County History: Wiltshire* i, pt 1, 21–279.
Hawkes, S.C. & Dunning, G.C., 1961.	'Soldiers and Settlers in Britain, fourth to fifth century', *Medieval Archaeol.* v, 1–71.
Leech, R.H., 1973.	'Excavations at Catsgore', *Somerset Archaeol. Natural History* cxvii, 115–6.
Leech, R.H., 1975.	*Small Medieval Towns in Avon: Archaeology and Planning* (Bristol).
Ministry of Public Building & Works, 1962.	*Excavations Annual Report* (London).
Ministry of Public Building & Works, 1963.	*Excavations Annual Report* (London).
Ministry of Public Building & Works, 1966.	*Excavations Annual Report* (London).
Ministry of Public Building & Works, 1969.	*Archaeological Excavations 1968* (London).
Ministry of Public Building & Works, 1970.	*Archaeological Excavations 1969* (London).
Myres, J.N.L., 1969.	*Anglo-Saxon Pottery and the Settlement of England* (Oxford).
O'Neill, H.E., 1952.	'Whittington Court Roman Villa, Whittington, Gloucestershire', *Trans. Bristol Gloucestershire Archaeol. Soc.,* lxxi, 13–87.
O'Neill, H.E., & Grinsell, L.V., 1960.	'Gloucestershire Barrows', *Trans. Bristol Gloucestershire Archaeol. Soc.* lxxix, 1–149.
Piggott, S., 1973.	'The Beginnings of Human Settlement . . . . (to) . . . . The Final phase of Bronze Technology', *Victoria County History: Wiltshire* i, pt 2, 281–407.
Royal Commission on Historical Monuments (England), 1960.	*A Matter of Time* (London).
Royal Commission on Historical Monuments (England), forthcoming.	*An Inventory of Ancient and Historical Monuments in Gloucestershire, i: Iron Age and Romano–British Monuments in the Cotswold Area* (London).
Rennie, D.M., 1971.	'Excavations in the Parsonage Field, Cirencester', *Trans. Bristol Gloucestershire Archaeol. Soc.* xc, 64–94.
Richmond, I.A., 1959.	'The Roman Villa at Chedworth', *Trans. Bristol Gloucestershire Archaeol. Soc.* lxxviii, 5–23.
Richmond, I.A. & Taylor, M.V., 1958.	'Roman Britain in 1957', *J. Rom. Stud.* xlviii, 130–149.
Richmond, I.A. & Taylor, M.V., 1959.	'Roman Britain in 1958', *J. Rom. Stud.* xlix, 102–135.
Richmond, I.A. & Taylor, M.V., 1960.	'Roman Britain in 1959', *J. Rom. Stud.* l, 210–236.

Richmond, I.A. & Wilson, D.R., 1961.	'Roman Britain in 1960. Sites explored', *J. Rom. Stud.* 1i, 156–191.
Riley, D.N., 1944.	'Archaeology from the air in the Upper Thames Valley', *Oxoniensia* viii–ix, 64–101.
Smith, I.F., 1972.	'Ring ditches in eastern and central Gloucestershire' in Fowler, P.J. (ed.), *Archaeology and the Landscape* (London), 157–67.
Tratman, E.K., 1970.	'The Glastonbury Lake Village: A Reconsideration', *Proc, Univ. Bristol Spelaeol. Soc.* xii, 143–167.
Wainwright, G.J., 1968.	'The Excavation of a Durotrigian Farmstead near Tollard Royal in Cranbour Chase, Southern England', *Proc. Prehist. Soc.* xxxiv, 102–147.
Wainwright, G.J. & Spratling, M., 1973.	'The Iron-Age Settlement of Gussage All Saints', *Antiquity* x1viii, 109–130.
Webster, G., 1967.	'Excavations at the Romano-British Villa in Barnsley Park, Cirencester 1961–66', *Trans. Bristol Gloucestershire Archaeol. Soc.* 1xxxvi, 74–87.
Webster, G., 1969.	'Cirencester: Dyer Court Excavation, 1957', *Trans. Bristol Gloucestershire Archaeol. Soc.* 1xxxviii, 44–85.
Wedlake, W.J., 1958.	*Excavations at Camerton* (Camerton)
Williams, R.G.B., 1973.	'Frost and the Works of Man', *Antiquity* xivii, 19–31.
Wilson, D.R., 1962.	'Roman Britain in 1961', *J. Rom. Stud.* 1ii, 160–190.
Wilson, D.R., 1963.	'Roman Britain in 1962', *J. Rom. Stud.* 1iii, 125–159.
Wilson, D.R., 1964.	'Roman Britain in 1963', *J. Rom. Stud.* 1iv, 152–177.
Wilson, D.R., 1965.	'Roman Britain in 1964', *J. Rom. Stud.* 1v, 199–220.
Wilson, D.R., 1966.	'Roman Britain in 1965', *J. Rom. Stud.* 1vi, 196–217.
Wilson, D.R., 1967.	'Roman Britain in 1966', *J. Rom. Stud.* 1vii, 174–202.
Wilson, D.R., 1968.	'Roman Britain in 1967, *J Rom. Stud.* 1viii, 176–206.
Wilson, D.R., 1969.	'Roman Britain in 1968', *J. Rom. Stud.* 1ix, 198–234.
Wilson, D.R., 1970.	'Roman Britain in 1969', *Britannia* i, 269–305.
Wilson, D.R., 1971.	'Roman Britain in 1970', *Britannia* ii, 243–288.
Wilson, D.R., 1972.	'Roman Britain in 1971', *Britannia* iii, 299–351.
Wilson, D.R., 1973.	'Roman Britain in 1972', *Britannia* iv, 271–323.